# Barbecu BIBLE

# Barbecue
# BIBLE

**Bounty**
**Books**

First published in Great Britain in 2003 by Hamlyn,
a division of Octopus Publishing Group Ltd

This edition published in 2013 by Bounty Books,
a division of Octopus Publishing Group Ltd,
Endeavour House, 189 Shaftesbury Avenue,
London WC2H 8JY
www.octopusbooks.co.uk

An Hachette UK Company
www.hachette.co.uk

ISBN: 978-0-753724-92-7

A CIP catalogue record for this book is available from the British Library

Printed in China

notes

Both metric and imperial measurements have been given in all recipes. Use
one set of measurements only, and not a mixture of both.

Standard level spoon measurements are used in all recipes.
1 tablespoon = one 15 ml spoon
1 teaspoon = one 5 ml spoon

Eggs should be large unless otherwise stated. The Department of Health
advises that eggs should not be consumed raw. This book contains dishes made
with raw or lightly cooked eggs. It is prudent for more vulnerable people such
as pregnant and nursing mothers, invalids, the elderly, babies and young
children to avoid uncooked or lightly cooked dishes made with eggs. Once
prepared, these dishes should be kept refrigerated and used promptly.

Milk should be full fat unless otherwise stated.

This book includes dishes made with nuts and nut derivatives. It is advisable
for customers with known allergic reactions to nuts and nut derivatives and
those who may be potentially vulnerable to these allergies, such as pregnant
and nursing mothers, invalids, the elderly, babies and children to avoid dishes
made with nuts and nut oils. It is also prudent to check the labels of pre-
prepared ingredients for the possible inclusion of nut derivatives.

# Contents

Notes for American readers

| UK | US | UK | US |
|---|---|---|---|
| aubergine | eggplant | jacket potato | baked potato |
| back fat | fatback | jug | pitcher |
| batavia lettuce | escarole | King prawn | jumbo shrimp |
| beetroot | beets | kitchen paper | paper towels |
| broad bean | fava bean | lemon/lime/ | lemon/lime/ |
| caster sugar | superfine sugar | orange rind | orange zest |
| Chinese leaves | Napa cabbage | mince/minced meat | ground meat |
| clingfilm | plastic wrap | muscavado sugar | brown sugar |
| cocktail sticks | toothpicks | natural yogurt | plain yogurt |
| coriander | cilantro | peppers | bell peppers |
| corn cobs | corn on the cob | petrol | gasoline |
| corn salad | mâche | plain flour | all-purpose flour |
| Cos lettuce | romaine lettuce | prawns | shrimp |
| courgettes | zucchini | preheated grill | preheated broiler |
| digestive biscuits | graham crackers | rapeseed oil | canola oil |
| double cream | heavy cream | rocket | arugula |
| fromage frais | fromage blanc | serviettes | paper napkins |
| full-fat milk | whole milk | single cream | light cream |
| grainy buns | multigrain buns | soured cream | sour cream |
| ground almonds | blanched almonds, ground fine | spring onions | scallions |
| | | stem ginger | crystallized ginger |
| groundnut oil | peanut oil | streaky bacon | sliced bacon |
| haricot bean | navy bean | sultanas | golden raisins |
| icing sugar | confectioner's sugar | sweetcorn | corn |
| | | vanilla pod | vanilla bean |

# Introduction

Barbecuing is an enjoyable and relaxing way to prepare a meal and brings family and friends together. And because it is such a simple way of cooking, everyone can join in. At the first whiff of a live flame everyone wants to get involved with preparing the meal, even if it is just to offer the benefit of their wide barbecuing experience.

Barbecuing over coals is also a healthy way of cooking which makes food look and taste good. Somehow food always seems to taste better if it has been cooked out-of-doors, and there is the added bonus of the tantalizing aromas to add to the anticipation.

Many different types of food are suitable for barbecuing and barbecues are great for a whole host of different occasions, whether it is a weekend brunch with all your neighbours, an intimate supper for two al fresco, a sophisticated dinner for friends or a lunchtime feast for all the family. The barbie really lends itself to entertaining – it is probably the combination of hot, sizzling food, cool crisp salads, chilled drinks and the relaxed feeling of the great outdoors. So get everyone together and start sizzling.

## Choosing a Barbecue

There are many styles of barbecue on offer, but before you start to look, ask yourself the following questions.

**How much room have you got?** It's not just a case of having enough space to accommodate the barbecue when it is in use, but you will also have to fit in somewhere to store it.

**How often are you likely to use a barbecue?** Answer this question truthfully before deciding how much money to spend on one. Some models are very expensive, but well worth it if you do lots of barbecuing. Others are much cheaper and perfectly suited to occasional use.

**Do you entertain on a large scale, or is it just close family?** This will help you decide how large a barbecue to get. The cooking area available will be a major factor if you frequently cook for lots of people.

**Portable or built-in?** Portable barbecues can be moved around the garden to take advantage of the best weather conditions. They can also be taken to the beach or on a picnic for those days out. However, you will have to find somewhere to store them when not in use. Built-in barbecues cannot be moved, but many people prefer to design their gardens with a barbecue as an integral part. Built-in barbecues are often more elaborate, with work surfaces, a chimney and storage space included.

## Barbecue Styles

**Kettle barbecues** are a compact, circular shape. They have a built-in domed lid, making them good for both grilling and roasting. They are best for cooking whole fish or large pieces of meat as they turn into a kind of oven when they have the lid on. You can't usually adjust the height of the grill rack above the coals so they are not very good for fine-tuning the temperature when grilling. Kettle barbecues come in gas or traditional charcoal. With the lid on, you can use smoking wood chips to flavour the food very successfully.

**Basic braziers** are either rectangular or round, and consist of a simple open grill on legs or wheels. Choose a well-made model if it is to last; there are lots of very cheap ones around which will soon warp or rust. Make sure the barbecue has adjustable cooking heights to make cooking easier.

**Hibachi** (the word means 'fire box' in Japanese) is a small cast-iron grill on very short legs. They are not very big but they are very sturdy. These are ideal for couples and small families, and their size makes them perfect for taking on camping trips and so on. They are normally quite cheap, but last a long time.

**Built-in barbecues** are versatile as they can be tailor-made to suit your needs. There are kits available to make building more straightforward. They are usually set in brick, either freestanding or built into a wall as part of the patio area. Many have work space on either side and built-in storage for accessories. If you cook outside often, consider building one with a chimney to funnel the smoke away while you are cooking.

**Gas barbecues** are generally in the style of a trolley, with space to store the gas bottle and barbecue utensils. Usually they have a small work surface either side. Make sure the one you choose has a sturdy frame and strong wheels for easy manoeuvring. Most models have a drip tray to catch the fat that drips off food – make sure it is easy to remove and clean. Ceramic rocks or lava rocks are used between the gas jets and the grill to conduct heat towards the food in an even manner. They last a long time but will eventually need to be replaced. Some gas barbecues have a normal grill section and also a solid hotplate for griddling foods.

## Fuel

There are three options for fuel – charcoal, wood or gas – and everyone has their own idea of which is best.

**Charcoal** comes in two forms: natural lumpwood charcoal and manufactured briquettes. In both cases it is worth buying a good-quality brand as it will burn for much longer. Lumpwood charcoal is easier to light than briquettes, which are denser and round or oval in shape. Both can be bought loose in sacks, or are available in special packages, usually four or five to the sack. You set light to the outside of the package, which in turn lights the charcoal. This is a very easy way to light a barbecue and does away with the need for firelighters or kindling.

**Wood** is less convenient as a barbecue fuel, but it can be very successful if you have some practice. You have to

# Where to Site a Barbecue

☀ A barbecue should be placed far enough away from the house so that the smoke doesn't blow in, but near enough to make carrying food and utensils easy.
☀ If you live in a windy position make sure the barbecue is protected from prevailing winds. A light breeze will actually help it burn if it is a still day, however, so you may want to move it around the garden to find the best spot before you light it.
☀ Site the barbecue well away from your neighbours so you don't irritate them with the smoke.
☀ Avoid placing the barbecue near dry shrubs or wooden fences which may catch light.
☀ Don't put a barbecue upwind of the dining table or you won't be able to see your guests while you are eating.

let the fire burn down to glowing embers before you can cook over wood, and this can take up to an hour. The heat output can be difficult to control once you start cooking, but you can adjust the heat by moving the food closer to or further away from the embers. Use hardwoods such as cherry, grapevines, apple, oak or olive.

**Gas** is quick and convenient, but it does not flavour the food as much as other fuels. Gas barbecues are more expensive to buy than charcoal or wood barbecues, and you have to remember to refill the gas bottle from time to time. Many people swear by their gas barbecues for the convenience they offer, but others feel that gas lacks the integrity and style of cooking over a real fire.

# Lighting Up

## To Light a Gas Barbecue

**1** Switch on the gas and light the barbecue about 15 minutes before you want to cook to allow the lava rocks to heat up evenly. Most gas models have an automatic ignition so you won't even need matches.

**2** When the coals are hot, brush a layer of oil on to the grill bars or hotplate to prevent the food from sticking. Apply it with kitchen paper or an old pastry brush.

## To Light a Charcoal Barbecue

**1** Start at least 30 minutes before you want to start cooking. Line the charcoal tray with kitchen foil to make it easier to clean afterwards. If you don't have self-lighting bags of charcoal, use firelighters or newspaper and dry twigs to get the fire going. There are also barbecue lighting fuels available, which you have to douse on the charcoal and leave for 10 minutes before lighting to allow it to soak in, but they aren't always sufficient to get the charcoal lit.

**2** Make a fire by layering charcoal with firelighters (or newspaper and twigs). Build a cone-shaped fire in the centre of the barbecue tray as it will catch more easily, and the embers can be spread out for cooking later. Use long matches to light the firelighters and leave the fire until the coals have burnt down to ash-coated embers.

**3** Spread out the embers to increase the cooking area, then put the grill rack in place. There should be no flames when you start cooking. Leave the grill bars to heat up, then oil them lightly with oil-soaked kitchen paper or an old pastry brush to prevent the food sticking.

**4** Top up the coals as you cook if you have lots of food to barbecue. Add new ones round the edges of the fire and, as they warm up, move a few at a time into the middle to burn.

ABOVE: There are many handy toold and accessories available to help with every barbecue need.

# Tools and Accessories

✸ **long-handled tongs:** useful for turning food and taking it on or off the grill. Use a second pair for the coals.

✸ **long pronged fork:** don't pierce food while it is cooking; this will remove precious juices and flavours and dry out the food. Use only towards the end of cooking to check if meat or poultry is cooked.

✸ **fish slice:** useful for turning burgers and vegetables.

✸ **extra-long matches:** make fire-lighting easier and safer.

✸ **apron:** essential to protect you and your clothes from splashing fat.

✸ **rubber gloves:** for handling black and messy coals when setting up the fire.

✸ **basting brush:** for basting food and oiling the grill.

ABOVE: You can pick up all sorts of barbecue trays that can be used for cooking smaller items of food that would otherwise fall through the grill.

✳ **wire brush:** perfect for cleaning messy grill racks.

✳ **vine clippings, mesquite chippings** or **hickory chips:** to add to the coals and flavour foods. Soak them in water for an hour beforehand so they burn more slowly and release more smoke.

✳ **bunches of woody herbs:** rosemary or thyme can be added to the fire to release aromatic smoke.

✳ **hinged baskets for fish:** these close tightly around the fish and have a handle for easy turning.

✳ **drip tray:** heavy-duty aluminium foil or a metal freezer tray can be placed on the coals under the food to catch the juices for use in a sauce, or to baste the food. This will also prevent flare-ups caused by dripping fat.

✳ **metal skewers:** help to hold foods flat for even cooking, and make turning lots of small pieces of food much easier and prevent them dropping through the bars. They can be used again and again.

✳ **wooden skewers:** have the same uses as metal skewers but must be soaked in water for an hour before threading on the food to stop them burning.

✳ **sugar cane, lemon grass** or **branches of rosemary:** these can be used as flavour-imparting skewers.

✳ **aluminium foil:** to wrap food before cooking, to keep it warm and to make a drip tray (see above).

# Caring for Your Barbecue

The main consideration is to keep the barbecue in a dry place while it is not in use. This will prevent it rusting and greatly extend its useful life. It is possible to buy a special barbecue cover to keep it clean. Make sure you store the charcoal somewhere dry too.

## To Clean a Gas Barbecue

**1** Scour the grill bars with a wire brush straight after removing the food, then turn the gas up to high for a few minutes to burn off the remaining food bits stuck to the bars. If you have used the hotplate, scrape off the bits of food with a wallpaper scraper (reserved just for the barbecue).

**2** Next, use kitchen paper to wipe over all the surfaces. When the barbecue has cooled down, wipe the grill bars and hotplate with oil-soaked kitchen paper to grease it, then cover it up and store it away.

## To Clean a Charcoal Barbecue

**1** Allow the barbecue to cool completely before cleaning it. When it is cold, remove the ash tray and dispose of the ash. Remove the grill rack and clean it gently with a wire brush.

**3** Wash the inside and outside of the barbecue and dry it with newspaper. Wipe the grill rack with oil-soaked kitchen paper, cover and store in a dry place.

# What to Cook

Most foods can be cooked on a barbecue, but some items are simply fantastic when cooked over coals, such as juicy steaks, flame-grilled burgers, succulent flavoursome sardines, charred sweet peppers and haloumi cheese. What you choose to cook will depend on the occasion, but most people use a barbecue as an excuse to serve many different things all together – perhaps some sausages in buns, some barbecue ribs, a few chicken drumsticks, pork chops and some vegetable kebabs. Everyone can help themselves to whatever they fancy, accompanied by a few simple salads and sauces. However, don't feel you have to serve so much every time you light the barbecue; you can make a delicious meal by having an impromptu barbecue (see pages 80–1) and cooking whatever you had planned for dinner.

## Poultry

Chicken, turkey, duck, guinea fowl, quail and any other small birds all lend themselves to barbecuing as it seals the flesh, crisps up the skin and imparts great flavour, resulting in juicy and delicious meat. Poultry can take on a whole host of different flavourings, from simple garlic and herbs to tandoori, Thai or Jamaican. Try Lemon and Herb Chicken Wings (see page 30–1), Duck Breasts with Caramelized Olives and Oranges (see page 67) or Partridges with Port and Grape Sauce (see page 89).

The fattier cuts and types of poultry are the best for barbecuing, such as chicken thighs, turkey wings and duck, as they baste themselves while they cook and stay moist. Boneless breast fillets don't take long to cook, but you must be careful not to overcook them and let them dry out. Drumsticks, wings and thighs are popular cuts as the meat is juicy and moist, but make sure they are cooked right through as they have a bone in them and will take much longer.

For a special occasion, consider cooking the birds whole. Smaller birds, such as quail, partridge or poussin, can be barbecued as they come. Larger birds are better if they are spatchcocked first, which involves removing the

> **Poultry Sizzling Times**
> Boneless chicken breasts  12 minutes
> Boneless duck breasts  15 minutes
> Chicken thighs (with bone)  20 minutes
> Chicken drumsticks  25 minutes
> Chicken or turkey wings  20 minutes
> Spatchcocked chicken or guinea fowl  35 minutes
> Whole partridge  15–20 minutes
> Spatchcocked poussin  25 minutes

backbone and flattening the bird to reduce the cooking time. A lid will also speed up cooking and keep the meat moist. A kettle barbecue comes with a solid lid and lends itself to cooking large pieces of meat or poultry, but a piece of kitchen foil will also make a suitable lid if you don't have a kettle barbecue.

## Meat

To many people, a barbecue is not a barbecue without a juicy steak, chargrilled on the outside and juicy pink within. In fact, barbecuing is the perfect way to cook steaks. Don't spoil good meat with too much flavouring, let it speak for itself – a touch of garlic, some black pepper or a smear of mustard is all that is needed. If you are cooking for guests, ask them how they like their steak and cook to order.

Barbecues could likewise have been invented for burgers. Homemade burgers are by far the best (see page 18), and it is simple to vary the ingredients by adding a little finely chopped onion, some garlic, some chopped herbs and so on. Lamb mince makes great burgers, too, and pork patties can be made in the same way.

Lamb cutlets and lamb steaks are great for the barbecue as they are fatty enough to stay moist and succulent – keep the cutlets pink in the middle to retain their juiciness. Pork chops, fillet and ribs are also good for barbecuing as they have a good proportion of fat to

## Meat Sizzling Times

**Steak** 8–12 minutes, depending on thickness
  rare 3–4 minutes
  medium rare 4–5 minutes
  medium 5–6 minutes
  medium well done 6–8 minutes
  well done 8–12 minutes
**Lamb steaks** 6–8 minutes
**Lamb cutlets** 8 minutes
**Boned leg of lamb** 30 minutes
**Pork chops** 20 minutes
**Pork ribs** 15 minutes
**Sausages** 15 minutes
**Burgers, thin** 8–10 minutes
**Burgers, thick** 12–15 minutes

## How to Cook the Perfect Sausage

**1** Allow sausages to come to room temperature before cooking.
**2** Never prick the skins as it allows the juices to run out.
**3** Cook over medium coals – never hot – to stop the skins bursting.
**4** Alternatively, cook briefly in boiling water first to prevent the skins splitting on the barbecue.
**5** Cook slowly to avoid burning them as sausages blacken very easily.

keep the meat moist during cooking. Lamb and pork are both good for marinating as the meat is gutsy enough to take on strong flavourings. Pork is especially good with Asian Flavours. Try Hanoi Grilled Pork (see page 105) or Spicy Asian Pork Chops (see page 70).

Pork also makes that other great favourite of the barbie: the sausage. You can either make your own (see page 16) or buy good-quality ready-made sausages from a butcher. There are many different flavours around, so experiment to find the best.

## Cooking Meat

✳ When cooking large pieces of meat, or to speed up cooking, cover the food with a lid. A piece of kitchen foil or a wok lid is a good standby if you don't have a kettle barbecue with its own lid.

✳ When cooking meat, cook for longer on the first side and turn it over just once. You can rotate the meat once on each side if the heat is uneven.

✳ Don't cut into meat to see if it is cooked as it will lose all its juices.

✳ Bring meat to room temperature before cooking as it is easier to control the rate of cooking if it is not chilled.

✳ Avoid overcooking good meat such as steak or duck breast – it will make it dry and tough.

✳ Allow meat to rest before serving. Keep it somewhere warm for 5–10 minutes before carving or serving. This includes steak, lamb and pork fillets, chops and larger pieces of meat.

## Fish and Seafood

Fish cooks quickly and is simply delicious cooked over coals. Try firm white fish fillets such as monkfish, oily fish steaks like tuna or swordfish, or small whole fish like sardines or mackerel. For a special occasion, cook a large whole fish, such as a salmon or sea bass; cover it as it cooks using a lid or kitchen foil, to keep the flesh moist and speed up cooking. Fish fillets or whole fish can be wrapped in kitchen foil or banana leaves during cooking. This will keep them moist and make them easier to turn. Try Salmon and Samphire en Papillote (see page 94) or Sizzling Fish in Banana Leaves (see page 114). Fish can be simply enhanced with a few herbs and a little oil or butter, or try Oriental flavours such as garlic, ginger and lemon grass for a more exotic dish.

Many types of seafood can be barbecued. Squid, scallops and prawns are particularly successful as they are well suited to the quick, hot sear of a barbecue and take on wonderful chargrilled flavours.

## Vegetables

Barbecued vegetables make great accompaniments to meat, but they are also delicious and satisfying in their own right. The choice ranges from lightly charred asparagus spears served with melted butter, crispy potato wedges or silky slices of aubergine, to whole open-cap mushrooms or slices of courgette basted with garlic. See pages 140–1 for more tips and information about barbecuing fruit and vegetables.

To make sure vegetarians feel welcome, try more substantial dishes such as burgers made from red beans and rice (see page 125) or koftas made from nuts and served with minted yogurt (see page 130). Stuffed peppers are also popular (see pages 26), but whatever you decide to cook, be sure to cook vegetarian food separately from any meat you may be cooking.

## Testing the Heat

Grilling or barbecuing is carried out over high, medium or low heat depending on the kind of food. It is easy to adjust the heat on gas barbecues and kettle ones with adjustable vents. To test the temperature of the more common open grid barbecue, place your hand carefully a few centimetres or inches above the coals. If you can keep you hand there for;

**5 seconds** – then the heat is low
**3–4 seconds** – the heat is medium
**2 seconds** – the heat is high.

The right height for barbecuing is about 5–7.5cm (2–3 inches) above the grid. If the coals have become too hot for certain foods, then position the food away from the centre of the barbecue.

## Marinating Times

Marinades will transform basic meat, fish or vegetable dishes into something special. If you are short of time, however, don't worry about marinating for as long as the recipe specifies, just do it for as long as you've got. Many marinades can be made from basic or storecupboard ingredients, such as Herb Marinade (see page 182), Soy Sauce Marinade (see page 182), Hoisin Marinade (see page 182), Coconut Cream Marinade (see page 183), Barbecue Marinade (see page 183), Vermouth Marinade (see page 183) and Sweet and Sour Marinade (see page 183).

## Desserts

Sweet barbecued foods may sound odd to the uninitiated, but many fruits can be barbecued to perfection, giving them a wonderful caramelized flavour. Whole bananas, still in their skins, can be popped on to the barbecue when you have finished cooking the main course, and will bake away gently as you eat your dinner. When cooked through, they are soft and succulent, perfect with ice cream, sorbet or cream and sugar. Many other fruits are also perfect for barbecuing: pineapple, mango and apples are just a few. See pages 162–7 for a selection of delicious barbecued dessert recipes.

# Barbecuing Hints

✹ Marinate to add extra excitement to plain meat and vegetables. See the marinade recipes on pages 182–3.

✹ Avoid cooking very fatty foods on a barbecue as they drip fat on to the coals. This causes flare-ups, which blacken food and give it a burnt flavour.

✹ Sizzling times will vary from barbecue to barbecue, from fuel to fuel, and will be longer on a windy day.

✹ Adjust the height of the grill to adjust the heat. Start by searing the food close to the coals to seal it, then move the rack up to finish cooking at a lower temperature.

✹ Alternatively, move the coals apart to lower the heat and pile them up closer together to increase the heat.

✹ Make sure you have enough charcoal to finish cooking all the food.

# Safety Tips

★ Don't barbecue in bare feet.
★ Never use petrol, paraffin or other flammable liquids to light the fire.
★ Make sure the barbecue is stable and won't topple over when lit.
★ Keep children and pets under control.
★ Never leave a barbecue unattended.
★ Have a bucket of water or a hose to hand just in case.
★ Leave the coals to cool completely before touching them or cleaning the barbecue.
★ Never leave raw meat or fish in full sun. Keep it cool until you are ready to cook.
★ Make sure pork and chicken are cooked right through before serving. If you are worried about this, choose boneless meat as it will cook through much more quickly.
★ Don't put cooked food back on to the plates on which you brought out the raw food.
★ When basting meat with a brush during cooking, be sure not to use the same brush on both raw and cooked or nearly cooked foods.

# Don't Forget!

The cooking times given in the recipes are a guide only. There are many variables with barbecue cooking, from the thickness of the food to the heat of the coals.

# chapter 1
# Top Ten Favourites

All your favourite barbecue foods are included in this top ten list, from Homemade Sausages with Mustard Aioli to Peppered Chicken Skewers. These popular recipes with a twist will form the basis of a perfect summer barbecue.

# Homemade Sausages with Mustard Aioli

**Preparation time:** 30 minutes
**Cooking time:** 10–15 minutes

Serves 4

sausage casings
500 g (1 lb) lean shoulder pork
175 g (6 oz) back fat without rind
1½ tablespoons coarse sea salt
4 tablespoons fresh thyme leaves
½ teaspoon ground bay
pepper

**1** Soak the casings in cold water for 20 minutes, untangle knots, then rinse by pulling one end of the casing over the end of the tap and running cold water through it.

**2** Trim any skin or gristle from the shoulder and back fat and cut into pieces. Pass the meat through the medium blade of a mincer or, alternatively, finely chop it by hand. Place the meat in a large bowl and add the back fat, sea salt, thyme, bay and pepper. Mix well.

**3** Spoon the meat into a large piping bag filled with a large plastic nozzle and squeeze to remove any excess air. Wriggle the open end of a casing on to and up the nozzle and, holding the skin on to the nozzle, squeeze the filling into the casing to create a long sausage. Twist or knot the long sausage at intervals to make 8 large or 12 small sausages.

**4** Place the sausages on the barbecue grill over a fairly low heat and cook, turning frequently, for 10–15 minutes until cooked through. Serve hot with the aioli.

## Mustard Aioli

**Preparation time:** 30 minutes
**Cooking time:** 10–15 minutes

Serves 4

4–6 garlic cloves, crushed
2 egg yolks
2 tablespoons lemon juice, plus extra to taste
300 ml (½ pint, 1¼ cups) extra virgin olive oil
2 tablespoons coarse grain mustard
salt and pepper

**1** Place the garlic and egg yolks in a blender or food processor, add the lemon juice and process briefly to mix. With the motor running, gradually add the olive oil in a thin stream until the mixture forms a thick cream. Scrape the aioli into a bowl, season and stir in the mustard, adding more lemon juice if needed.

**barbie tip**
Use the sausage-meat mixture to make small patties rather than sausages with skins, if you prefer. Cook these as you would burgers.

# Spicy Burgers 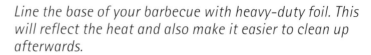 2

*Line the base of your barbecue with heavy-duty foil. This will reflect the heat and also make it easier to clean up afterwards.*

**Preparation time:** 15 minutes
**Cooking time:** 6–10 minutes

Makes 8

1 kg (2 lb) minced beef
2 tablespoons green peppercorns
1 tablespoon chopped thyme
2 teaspoons Worcestershire sauce
2 teaspoons French mustard
salt

To serve:
8 burger buns
8 lettuce leaves
selection of relishes
1 onion, sliced
4 tomatoes, sliced

**1** Put the beef in a bowl and season well with salt. Stir in the peppercorns, thyme, Worcestershire sauce and mustard, and mix well. Divide into 8 portions and form into flat burgers.

**2** Cook the burgers on an oiled barbecue grill 10 cm (4 inches) above the coals for 3–5 minutes on each side, according to taste.

**3** Cut the buns in half and toast the cut side. Arrange a lettuce leave on each bun base, top with a burger and relish. Arrange onion and tomato slices on top and replace the bun lid. Serve immediately.

**barbie tip**
Hinged baskets make turning these homemade beefburgers much easier.

# Balsamic Steaks with Basil Mash ③

*Rich, dark, Italian balsamic vinegar is used in a marinade for barbecued fillet steaks. The mashed potatoes are flavoured with basil oil.*

**Preparation time:** 20 minutes, plus marinating
**Cooking time:** 30 minutes

**Serves 4**

4 fillet steaks, about 250 g (8 oz) each
2 red onions, thinly sliced into rings
3 tablespoons balsamic vinegar
50 ml (2 fl oz, ¼ cup) red wine
150 ml (¼ pint, ⅔ cup) olive oil
1–2 garlic cloves, crushed
50 g (2 oz, 2 cups) basil leaves
1 kg (2 lb) potatoes, cut into large chunks
salt and pepper

**1** Place the steaks in a shallow dish large enough to hold them in a single layer. Sprinkle the red onion rings over the top. Mix the balsamic vinegar in a jug with the red wine and 2 tablespoons of the olive oil. Add the garlic and pour over the steaks. Turn to coat, cover the dish and marinate for 1–1½ hours, turning once.

**2** Place the basil leaves in a blender or food processor with the remaining olive oil. Process until smooth, then pour into a bowl and set aside.

**3** Cook the potatoes in lightly salted water for 15–20 minutes, until tender. Drain well, return to the pan and place over the heat for a few minutes to dry off any excess moisture. Shake the pan frequently to prevent burning. Mash the potatoes in the pan while still warm. Stir in the basil oil and season with a little salt and plenty of pepper. Cover with a snug-fitting lid to keep warm.

**4** Remove the meat from the dish, cover and set aside. Tip the marinade, including the onions, into a saucepan. Bring to the boil, then reduce the heat and simmer until it is reduced by about half. Place the pan on the side of the barbecue to keep warm while you cook the steaks.

**5** Cook the steaks on an oiled barbecue grill over hot coals for 2–3 minutes on each side for very rare, 3–4 minutes on each side for rare, 4–5 minutes for medium rare. Spoon over the sauce and serve with the basil-flavoured mashed potatoes

**barbie tip**
Serve a tomato salad scattered with chopped spring onions with the steaks to complete the meal.

# Tandoori Chicken

Preparation time: 20 minutes, plus marinating
Cooking time: 30 minutes

Serves 4

1 hot red chilli, deseeded and roughly chopped
2 garlic cloves, roughly chopped
2.5 cm (1 inch) piece of fresh root ginger, roughly chopped
2 tablespoons lemon juice
1 tablespoon coriander seeds
1 tablespoon cumin seeds
2 teaspoons garam masala
6 tablespoons natural yogurt
a few drops each of red and yellow food colouring
4 skinned chicken portions
salt

To garnish:
lemon wedges
coriander sprigs

**1** Put the chilli, garlic, ginger and lemon juice in an electric spice mill or food processor with the whole spices and garam masala, then work to a paste.

**2** Transfer the spice paste to a shallow dish in which the chicken portions will fit in a single layer. Add the yogurt, food colouring and salt and stir well to mix. Set aside.

**3** Score the flesh of the chicken deeply with a sharp pointed knife, cutting right down as far as the bone. Put the chicken in a single layer in the dish, then spoon the marinade over the chicken and brush it into the cuts in the flesh. Cover and marinate in the refrigerator for at least 4 hours, but preferably overnight.

**4** Cook the chicken over hot coals, turning frequently, for 30 minutes or until the juices run clear when pierced with a skewer or fork. Serve hot, garnished with lemon wedges and coriander sprigs.

### barbie tip
Make Tandoori Lamb in the same way, using 750 g (1½ lb) cubed shoulder of lamb instead of the chicken. Thread the meat on to skewers before cooking.

# Peppered Chicken Skewers with Rosemary

**Preparation time:** 10 minutes, plus marinating
**Cooking time:** 8–10 minutes

Serves 4

4 boneless, skinless chicken breasts
2 tablespoons finely chopped rosemary
2 garlic cloves, finely chopped
3 tablespoons lemon juice
2 teaspoons prepared English mustard
1 tablespoon clear honey
2 teaspoons freshly ground black pepper
1 tablespoon olive oil
salt
mixed leaf salad, to serve

**1** Lay a chicken breast between 2 sheets of cling film, then flatten it slightly with a mallet or rolling pin. Cut the chicken into thick strips. Repeat with the remaining chicken breasts.

**2** Put the chicken strips in a large shallow bowl. Add all the remaining ingredients and mix well. Cover and set aside to marinate for 5–10 minutes.

**3** Thread the chicken strips on to 8 metal skewers and cook for 4–5 minutes on each side or until the chicken is cooked through. Serve at once with a mixed leaf salad.

**barbie tip**
To create Greek Chicken Kebabs, substitute the rosemary with chopped thyme leaves and omit the English mustard. Serve with a feta cheese and tomato salad.

# Grilled Sardines with Chilli Oil

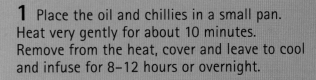

**6**

**Preparation time:** 15 minutes, plus infusing
**Cooking time:** 6–8 minutes

Serves 4

125 ml (4 fl oz, ½ cup) olive oil
2 tablespoons chopped dried red chillies
12 small sardines, cleaned and scaled
coarse sea salt

To SERVE:
lemon wedges
crusty bread
tomato and onion salad

**1** Place the oil and chillies in a small pan. Heat very gently for about 10 minutes. Remove from the heat, cover and leave to cool and infuse for 8–12 hours or overnight.

**2** Strain the oil through a sieve lined with muslin or a clean tea towel. Pour into a sterilized jar or bottle.

**3** Brush the sardines with a little of the chilli oil, sprinkle with coarse sea salt and cook on an oiled barbecue grill over hot coals for 6–8 minutes, or until just cooked, turning once. Serve immediately, with lemon wedges, crusty bread and a tomato and onion salad.

**barbie tip**
To save time, you can buy chilli oil but it tends to be hot. Mix just a few drops of bought chilli oil with 125 ml (4 fl oz, ½ cup) of olive oil.

# Tuna Niçoise

**Preparation time:** 20 minutes, plus marinating
**Cooking time:** 20 minutes

Serves 4

12 quails' eggs
500 g (1 lb) baby new potatoes
250 g (8 oz) fine French beans, topped and tailed
4 tuna steaks, about 175 g (6 oz) each
6 tablespoons olive oil
2 tablespoons chopped parsley
½ tablespoon lemon juice
2 tablespoons mixed whole peppercorns, crushed
125 g (4 oz, 1 cup) black olives, pitted
4 ripe tomatoes, quartered
12 canned anchovy fillets, drained
1 Cos lettuce
crusty bread, to serve

**barbie tip**
If you can't find quails' eggs, use 4 hens' eggs instead, and boil them for 5–8 minutes.

DRESSING:
1 garlic clove, crushed
1 tablespoon white wine vinegar
5 tablespoons olive oil

**1** Bring a pan of water to the boil. Add the quails' eggs, then lower the heat and simmer for 3 minutes. Refresh under cold running water, then shell the eggs.

**2** Boil the potatoes in lightly salted water for 10 minutes until just tender. Drain, refresh under cold running water and drain again.

**3** Blanch the French beans in a separate saucepan of boiling water for 3–4 minutes. Tip into a colander, refresh under cold water and drain again. Place the eggs and vegetables in separate bowls and set aside until required. Do not chill.

**4** Place the tuna steaks in a single layer in a shallow dish. Mix the olive oil, parsley, lemon juice and peppercorns in a jug. Pour the mixture over the fish, turning to coat all the steaks. Marinate for 30–60 minutes, turning once.

**5** Remove the tuna from the marinade and reserve the marinade. Cook the tuna on an oiled barbecue grill over hot coals for 3–4 minutes on each side, until just cooked, basting frequently with the marinade.

**6** Meanwhile, mix the potatoes, beans, olives, tomatoes, anchovies and lettuce in a large bowl. Place the dressing ingredients in a screw-top jar, close the lid and shake until well mixed. Pour the dressing over the bowl of salad and toss lightly. Top with the eggs and hot tuna steaks and serve with plenty of crusty bread.

# Coconut Butterfly Prawns

**Preparation time:** 10 minutes, plus marinating
**Cooking time:** 5–6 minutes

Serves 4

12 large raw tiger prawns in their shells
2 garlic cloves, crushed
1 cm (½ inch) piece of fresh root ginger, peeled and very finely shredded
2 tablespoons lime juice
1–2 red chillies, deseeded and finely chopped
150 ml (¼ pint, ⅔ cup) coconut cream

**barbie tip**

This spicy coconut marinade works equally well on scallops or cubes of monkfish or chicken.

**1** To prepare the prawns, first remove the legs and cut off the heads with a small sharp knife. Holding a prawn with the back uppermost, slice along its length, from the thickest part towards the tail, cutting almost but not quite through. Carefully remove the dark vein that runs down its back.

**2** Gently press the prawn to flatten it out and make the butterfly shape. Repeat with the remaining prawns and rinse well under running water. Pat the prawns dry on kitchen paper and place them in a large flat dish.

**3** Mix the garlic, ginger, lime juice, chillies and coconut cream in a jug. Pour the mixture over the prawns, turning to coat them well. Cover the dish and marinate for 1–2 hours.

**4** Drain the prawns and thread them on to 4 skewers. Cook on a well-oiled grill rack over moderately hot coals for 5–6 minutes, turning once, until the flesh is opaque and just cooked. Serve at once.

# Stuffed Mini Peppers with Tomato Sauce

*Miniature peppers, stuffed with a creamy minted cheese, are delicious with plain grilled chicken or as a starter.*

**Preparation time:** 20 minutes
**Cooking time:** 10–15 minutes

Serves 4

8 mini peppers
Greek yogurt, to serve

STUFFING:
125 g (4 oz) soft fresh goats' cheese
50 g (2 oz, ¼ cup) ricotta
1½ tablespoons chopped mint
1 red or green chilli, deseeded and finely chopped (optional)

**barbie tip**
Do not be tempted to fill the peppers completely, or they may burst during cooking.

TOMATO SAUCE:
1 tablespoon olive oil
1 onion, finely chopped
1 garlic clove, crushed
400 g (13 oz) can tomatoes
1 tablespoon chopped parsley
1 tablespoon chopped oregano

**1** To make the sauce, heat the oil in a saucepan, add the onion and the garlic and cook for 5 minutes, until softened but not coloured. Stir in the canned tomatoes and herbs and simmer gently for 10 minutes. Strain the sauce through a sieve set over a clean pan. Set aside.

**2** To make the stuffing, combine the goats' cheese, ricotta and mint in a bowl. Stir in the chilli, if using, and season to taste.

**3** Make a small slit in the side of each pepper, carefully scrape out the seeds and core with a teaspoon, keeping the pepper shells intact. Half-fill each pepper with stuffing.

**4** Cook the filled peppers on an oiled barbecue grill over moderately hot coals for about 10–15 minutes, turning occasionally, until softened. Meanwhile, reheat the tomato sauce by placing the pan at the edge of the barbecue grill. Serve the peppers with the sauce and some Greek yogurt.

# Potato Skins with Soured Cream

**Preparation time:** 15 minutes
**Cooking time:** 1½ hours

Makes 20

5 large baking potatoes, scrubbed and dried
150 ml (¼ pint, ⅔ cup) soured cream
1 teaspoon snipped chives
salt and pepper
vegetable oil, for brushing

**1** Prick the potatoes with a fork and bake in a preheated oven, 190°C (375°F), Gas Mark 5, for about 1¼ hours until tender.

**2** Meanwhile, prepare the dip. Mix the soured cream with the chives and salt and pepper to taste. Spoon into a bowl, cover and chill.

**3** Leave the potatoes to cool for a few minutes, then cut each one in half lengthways then again to make 4 long pieces. Using a teaspoon, scoop out most of the potato, leaving just a thin layer next to the skin. (Use the removed potato in another dish.)

**4** Brush the potato skins with oil, then cook them over hot coals for 5–7 minutes on each side until golden. Sprinkle lightly with salt and serve with the soured cream dip.

**barbie tip**
This recipe is equally delicious with sweet potatoes. Choose those with orange flesh as they are prettier.

# chapter 2

# Family Fun

Informal meals for the whole family which are quick and easy to prepare, including a guide on children's favourite barbecue foods and ideas for themed kid's parties.

# Lemon and Herb Chicken Wings

**Preparation time:** 5 minutes
**Cooking time:** 15–20 minutes

Serves 4

2 garlic cloves, crushed
grated rind and juice of 1 lemon
4 thyme sprigs
6 tablespoons olive oil
1 tablespoon clear honey
1 teaspoon dried oregano
1 teaspoon ground cumin
12 chicken wings
salt and pepper

**1** Put the garlic, lemon rind and juice into a bowl. Add the thyme leaves, oil, honey, oregano and cumin and season to taste with salt and pepper.

**2** Add the chicken wings and stir until well coated.

**3** Barbecue the chicken wings for 15–20 minutes, turning and basting until charred and cooked through.

**barbie tip**
Use the same mixture to coat chicken drumsticks or thighs, or try turkey portions instead.

# Chicken Satay

**Preparation time:** 10–15 minutes
**Cooking time:** 5 minutes

**Serves 4**

500 g (1 lb) chicken breast, thinly sliced into
    2.5 x 5 cm (1 x 2 inch) slices
Spicy Peanut Sauce (see page 185), to serve

MARINADE:
1 teaspoon ground cinnamon
1 tablespoon ground cumin
1 teaspoon ground black pepper
150 ml ($\frac{1}{4}$ pint, $\frac{2}{3}$ cup) oil
100 ml ($3\frac{1}{2}$ fl oz, $\frac{1}{2}$ cup) light soy sauce
2 tablespoons palm sugar or light muscovado sugar

TO GARNISH:
onion, roughly chopped
cucumber chunks

**1** Put the chicken slices into a bowl and add all marinade ingredients. Stir very thoroughly to make sure that all the chicken pieces are coated in the marinade. Leave for a minimum of 4 hours, but preferably overnight, giving it an occasional stir.

**2** Carefully thread the chicken pieces on to skewers, leaving some space at either end. Place them on a hot barbecue for about 5 minutes, turning once. As you cannot see if the chicken is cooked through, test one piece – you can always grill it for a little longer if necessary.

**3** Garnish with chopped raw onion and chunks of cucumber and serve with spicy peanut sauce.

### barbie tip
Make Pork Satay or King Prawn Satay in the same way, using the same quantity of thin slices of pork or large raw prawns in place of the chicken.

# Spatchcocked Poussins

**Preparation time:** 25 minutes
**Cooking time:** 15–20 minutes

Serves 4

3 sundried tomatoes in oil, drained and chopped, with oil reserved
125 g (4 oz, ½ cup) butter, softened
3 tablespoons roughly chopped basil
4 poussins, about 500 g (1 lb) each
salt and pepper

**1** Place the sundried tomatoes in a blender or food processor, add the butter, basil and seasoning and purée until smooth. Alternatively, finely chop the tomatoes and basil and beat with the butter in a bowl. Cover and chill.

**2** Place the poussins, one at a time, breast side down on a board and, using poultry shears or strong kitchen scissors, cut down either side of the backbone and remove it. Turn over and open out the poussin, then flatten by pressing down hard on the breastbone with the heel of your hand.

**3** Lift the skin covering the breast and gently push your fingers between the flesh and skin to create a pocket. Divide the butter equally between the poussins, pushing it underneath the skin.

**4** Working with one bird at a time, thread a skewer through a drumstick, under the breastbone and through the second drumstick. Thread another skewer through the wings, catching the flap of skin underneath. This will help to flatten the bird for even cooking. If using wooden skewers, soak them in cold water for about 30 minutes before using.

**5** Brush the poussins with the oil from the tomatoes and place on an oiled barbecue grill over hot coals. Cook for 15–20 minutes, until the juices run clear when the thickest part of a thigh is pierced with a skewer.

**barbie tip**
This method is ideal for barbecuing as it speeds up the cooking process and cooks the meat evenly.

# Turkey, Tomato and Tarragon Burgers

Preparation time: 20 minutes
Cooking time: 20–25 minutes

Serves 4

8 sundried tomato halves in oil, drained and chopped
500 g (1 lb) minced turkey
1 tablespoon chopped tarragon
½ red onion, finely chopped
½ teaspoon paprika
½ teaspoon salt
4 slices of smoked pancetta or rindless streaky bacon, halved

To serve:
4 ciabatta rolls
shredded radicchio and Cos lettuce

**1** Place the sundried tomatoes, turkey and tarragon in a blender or food processor and purée until smooth. Spoon the mixture into a bowl and stir in the onion. Season with the paprika and salt. Mix well, divide into 4 and shape into burgers. Stretch 2 strips of pancetta over each burger and secure with cocktail sticks.

**2** Barbecue the burgers over hot coals for 20–25 minutes, turning frequently. Serve at once in the ciabatta rolls with shredded radicchio and lettuce.

**barbie tip**
Soak the cocktail sticks in water for 30 minutes before use, as you would with skewers, to prevent them burning during cooking.

# Carnival Chicken with Sweet Potato Mash

**Preparation time:** 15–20 minutes, plus marinating
**Cooking time:** 20 minutes

**Serves 4**

4 skinless chicken breasts, about 150 g (5 oz) each
flat leaf parsley sprigs, to garnish

MARINADE:
100 ml (3½ fl oz, ½ cup) sweet sherry
1 teaspoon Angostura bitters
1 tablespoon light soy sauce
1 tablespoon chopped fresh root ginger
pinch of ground cumin
pinch of ground coriander
1 teaspoon dried mixed herbs
1 small onion, finely chopped
75 ml (3 fl oz, ⅓ cup) chicken stock

SWEET POTATO MASH:
2 sweet potatoes
2 tablespoons fromage frais
salt and pepper

**1** Place the chicken breasts in a non-metallic dish. In a bowl mix together all the marinade ingredients. Spoon over the chicken, making sure the pieces are well coated. Cover and marinate in the refrigerator overnight.

**2** When you are ready to cook, place the chicken on the barbecue and cook over medium coals for 20 minutes, turning over halfway through cooking.

**3** Meanwhile, boil the sweet potatoes in their skins for 20 minutes, until soft. Drain and peel. Mash the potato, let it dry off a bit then stir in the fromage frais. Season and serve with the chicken, garnished with parsley.

**barbie tip**
Children love this fragrant chicken and deliciously sweet potato mash, so it makes a great barbie dish for the family.

# Spare Ribs with Ginger

**Preparation time:** 10 minutes
**Cooking time:** 15–20 minutes

Serves 4–6

1 kg (2 lb) pork spare ribs

SAUCE:
2 spring onions, chopped
1 garlic clove, finely sliced
2.5 cm (1 inch) piece of fresh root ginger, shredded
1 tablespoon soy sauce
4 tablespoons clear honey
3 tablespoons lemon juice
2 tablespoons mango chutney
½ teaspoon ground ginger
1 tablespoon oil
2 tablespoons dry sherry

**1** Arrange the spare ribs on the barbecue 10 cm (4 inches) above hot coals and cook for 5 minutes, turning occasionally.

**2** Put all the sauce ingredients in a pan over a low heat, gradually bring to the boil and cook for 1 minute.

**3** Remove the ribs from the barbecue and place in a shallow dish. Spoon the sauce over the ribs, and turn to cover them all well. Return the ribs to the barbecue and cook for 10–15 minutes, basting frequently.

**barbie tip**
Make more of these sweet, sticky ribs than you think you could ever need – they seem to disappear rather fast.

# Lamb Cutlets with Rosemary and Lemon

Preparation time: 5 minutes, plus marinating
Cooking time: 10 minutes

Serves 4

juice and finely grated rind of ½ lemon
1 garlic clove, crushed
4 rosemary sprigs, finely chopped
4 anchovy fillets oil, drained and finely chopped
2 tablespoons extra virgin olive oil
2 tablespoons lemon cordial
12 lamb cutlets
salt and pepper
Sweet potato skins, to serve

1 Put the lemon rind and juice into a bowl and add the garlic, rosemary, anchovies, olive oil and lemon cordial. Mix thoroughly and add the lamb cutlets. Season with salt and pepper, turn to coat and set aside to marinade for 15 minutes.

2 Barbecue the lamb over hot coals for 3–5 minutes on each side, until charred and cooked through. Leave to rest for a few minutes and serve with barbecued sweet potato skins.

## Sweet Potato Skins

To prepare sweet potato skins, bake some sweet potatoes whole until soft right through. Cut them into quarters, scoop out some of the flesh, brush the skins with oil, season to taste with salt and pepper and barbecue the skins until crisp.

**barbie tip**
Trim as much fat as possible off the lamb before cooking. Excess fat will drip on the coals and cause flare-ups and burnt food.

# Pork Chops with Apple Sauce and Parsnips

Preparation time: 20 minutes, plus marinating
Cooking time: 20–25 minutes

Serves 4

4 apples, peeled
leaves from 1 rosemary sprig, finely chopped
2 tablespoons clear honey
½ tablespoon grated fresh root ginger
2 tablespoons water
4 pork chops or cutlets, about 325 g (11 oz) each
1 garlic clove, crushed
3 tablespoons olive oil
1 tablespoon sherry vinegar
500 g (1 lb) young parsnips
25 g (1 oz, 2 tablespoons) butter, melted
salt and pepper

**1** Slice each apple into 8 wedges and place in a saucepan with the rosemary, honey, ginger and water. Cover and bring to the boil, then lower the heat and simmer for 10–12 minutes, until the apples are tender. Leave the apple wedges whole or purée in a blender or food processor until smooth.

**2** Place the chops in a single layer in a shallow dish. Mix the garlic, olive oil, vinegar and seasoning in a jug, pour over the chops and turn to coat. Cover and leave to marinate for 1–2 hours.

**3** Peel the parsnips and cut them in half lengthways. Brush them with the melted butter and sprinkle with salt. Cook on an oiled barbecue grill over hot coals for 20–25 minutes, turning occasionally.

**4** When the parsnips have been cooking for about 10 minutes, drain the chops, reserving the marinade, and add them to the barbecue grill. Cook for 6–7 minutes each side, basting frequently with the marinade.

**5** Serve the chops with the grilled parsnips and the apple sauce.

**barbie tip**
Grilled asparagus also makes a delicious accompaniment to these chops. Cook the spears for 5–10 minutes, turning frequently, until lightly charred and tender.

# Fish Burgers with Yogurt Mayo

*Made by simply whizzing the ingredients together in a food processor, these mildly flavoured burgers are a good way of getting fussy eaters to enjoy fresh fish.*

**Preparation time:** 15 minutes, plus chilling
**Cooking time:** 6 minutes

Serves 4

500 g (1 lb) skinless cod or haddock fillet
4 spring onions, roughly chopped
1 egg white
50 g (2 oz, 1 cup) white breadcrumbs
2 tablespoons sunflower or vegetable oil
salt and pepper

To SERVE:
3 tablespoons Greek yogurt
3 tablespoons mayonnaise
4 grainy buns
salad leaves

**1** Check over the fish for any bones, then cut into pieces. Put the fish in a blender or food processor with the spring onions and process briefly until the ingredients are finely chopped. Add the egg white, breadcrumbs and a little salt and pepper, then process briefly until the ingredients are combined.

**barbie tip**
These fish burgers are also great served with jacket potatoes or with Barbecued Potato Wedges (see page 42).

**2** Divide the mixture into 4 portions and shape each one into a flat burger. (Wet the palms of your hands before shaping so that the mixture doesn't stick.) Chill the burgers for at least 1 hour before cooking.

**3** Brush the burgers with oil and place on an oiled barbecue rack over medium coals for about 3 minutes on each side until golden and firm.

**4** Meanwhile, mix together the yogurt, mayonnaise and a little salt and pepper. Split the buns and pile salad leaves on to each base. Put the burgers on top of the salad and add a spoonful of yogurt mayonnaise. Sandwich together with the burger tops and serve.

# Barbecued Potato Wedges with Sundried Tomato Aioli

**Preparation time:** 15–20 minutes
**Cooking time:** 20–25 minutes

**Serves 4**

4 large potatoes
4 tablespoons olive oil
paprika
sea salt flakes

SUNDRIED TOMATO AIOLI:
2–3 garlic cloves, crushed
2 egg yolks
about 2 tablespoons lemon juice
300 ml (½ pint, 1¼ cups) extra virgin olive oil
8 sundried tomato halves in oil, drained and finely chopped
salt and pepper

**1** Place the whole, unpeeled potatoes in a large pan of cold water, bring to the boil, reduce the heat and simmer for 15–20 minutes or until just tender. Drain, and when cool enough to handle, cut each potato into large wedges.

**2** To make the aioli, place the garlic and egg yolks in a blender or food processor, add the lemon juice and process briefly to mix. With the motor running, gradually add the oil in a thin stream until the mixture forms a thick cream. Scrape into a bowl and stir in the sundried tomatoes, season with salt and pepper, adding more lemon juice if liked.

**3** Brush the potato wedges with the oil, sprinkle with a little paprika and lay the potato wedges on the barbecue grill. Cook for 5–6 minutes, turning frequently until golden brown all over. Sprinkle with sea salt and serve with the aioli.

**barbie tip**
To make cooking and turning easier, the potato wedges can be threaded on to wooden or metal skewers.

# Mediterranean Kebabs

**Preparation time:** 20 minutes
**Cooking time:** 6–8 minutes

Serves 4

2 courgettes
12 cherry tomatoes
1 red onion, cut into 8 wedges
1 red pepper, cored, deseeded and cut into 2.5 cm
   (1 inch) squares
2 tablespoons olive oil
1 tablespoon finely chopped flat leaf parsley
4 tablespoons lemon juice
1 garlic clove, crushed
salt and pepper
chopped thyme, to garnish

**1** Trim the courgettes, then use a vegetable peeler to cut them lengthways into very thin slices or ribbons. Place the courgettes in a shallow bowl and add the tomatoes, onion and red pepper.

**2** Mix the oil, parsley, lemon juice, garlic and seasoning, then pour this mixture over the vegetables and set them aside to marinate for at least 5 minutes.

**3** Thread the vegetables on to 8 medium or 4 large metal skewers, making sure there is a variety of vegetables on each skewer and threading the strips of courgette between and around the other vegetables. Alternatively, you can roll up the courgette strips and thread the rolls on to the skewers. Reserve the juices from the marinade.

**4** Brush the vegetables with the reserved marinade and cook over medium coals, turning frequently, for about 6–8 minutes, until the vegetables are tender. Serve sprinkled with thyme.

**barbie tip**
These tasty kebabs can easily be adapted with a quick change of vegetables. Try using thick slices of fennel, cubes of aubergine and shiitake or button mushrooms.

# Children's Favourites

Barbecues are great for children of all ages. Most barbecue-friendly foods include kids' favourites, such as sausages, burgers and chicken pieces. If you have children who won't eat the same foods as adults, a barbecue is an easy way of serving up small amounts of different foods to keep everyone happy, and they can all be cooked together on the grill.

## Barbecues for Kids

Barbecues are perfect for children's parties, or even when they just have a few friends over, and it's easy to design a menu with them in mind. However, always remember to keep an eye on the children and keep them well away from the barbecue itself.

### The Burger Party

Serve a selection of burgers with buns, and lots of different toppings so each child can tailor-make their perfect burger. Provide grilled bacon, slices of cheese, relishes, sliced tomato, onion rings, mayonnaise and of course ketchup as toppings, with plenty of soft buns.

### The Wild West BBQ

Cowboy themes are always popular. Supply lots of different sausages for the kids to try, either homemade or bought. Serve the sausages in hotdog buns, with sauces and fried onions to be added as the children wish.

Baked beans make a suitable and enjoyable accompaniment. End the party with marshmallow toasting over the embers – provide plenty of wooden skewers and supervise at all times.

### Do-It-Yourself Kebabs

Kids love making up their own kebabs and deciding what to thread on to the skewers. Provide plenty of different ingredients, all cut into bite-sized pieces and presented in individual bowls. Include cherry tomatoes, squares of sweet peppers, chunks of sausage, meatballs (made from burger mixture), strips of chicken breast, button mushrooms, cubes of beef or pork, turkey chunks, apple wedges, chunks of courgette and haloumi cheese. Get an adult to cook the kebabs, remembering which one belongs to which child, and serve them with dips, salad and toasted pitta breads for filling. Sweet kebabs can make a great dessert – let them choose from banana chunks, marshmallows, strawberries or pineapple chunks.

### Fingerlickin' Ribs n' Wings

Spare ribs and chicken wings are great for chewing on the move, especially when the party is held in the garden. Marinate the ribs and wings before cooking to provide a selection of flavours, but include some plain ones for those fussy eaters. Serve with dips and sauces, plus barbecued potato wedges or skins and chunks of corn on the cob.

## Keeping Everyone Happy

Most of the recipes in this book can be adapted to suit children if necessary. In most cases, the strongly

# What Kids Like

✳ **Burgers** – either buy good-quality burgers, or make your own (see page 18), varying the ingredients from plain lamb or beef minces to minced chicken and turkey. Fish is another and rather less common option for tasty and nutritious burgers (see page 41).

✳ **Sausages** – these are another special favourite with kids. Like burgers, you can make your own (see page 16) and experiment with the ingredients as you like. Flavourings such as chopped apple, onion, herbs and spices always go down well. Sausages are a bit more fiddly to make than burgers, however, so you may just want to buy some good ones. Try out a variety of flavours at the same time as kids like to have a choice.

✳ **Kebabs** – these naturally appeal to kids as the meat and vegetables are cut into small bite-sized pieces, making them easy to eat.

✳ **Chicken wings and drumsticks** – these small cuts of meat are easy to pick up with the fingers and chew, making them popular with children of all ages. Try Lemon and Herb Chicken Wings (see pages 30–1), Cinnamon-spiced Chicken Wings (see page 58), or marinate the pieces in one of the many marinades.

✳ **Spare ribs** – another option for picking up with the fingers and chewing. Try Spare Ribs with Ginger (see page 37), or make barbecued spare ribs, using the Barbecue Marinade (see page 183).

✳ **Potato skins and wedges** – potatoes are always popular with kids, and crispy barbecued skins and wedges are especially appealing. Choose from Barbecued Potato Wedges with Sundried Tomato Aioli (see page 42) or Potato Skins with Soured Cream (see page 27).

✳ **Buns and bread rolls** – great accompaniments for burgers, sausages and kebabs.

✳ **Salad bits** – choose crunchy ingredients which can be picked up with the fingers such as cucumber and tomato chunks, apple slices and carrot sticks

✳ **Dips** – kids love dipping, so provide some mayonnaise, soured cream or a sauce, such as Basic Tomato Sauce (see page 185) or Spicy Peanut Sauce (see page 185).

✳ **Ketchup** – no barbecue is complete without the all-important ketchup. Most children, and many adults, will eat anything if they can dip it in ketchup.

flavoured ingredients can be left out of children's portions, while the adults enjoy them. For example, if you are marinating some chicken pieces in Thai flavourings, simply leave some pieces of chicken out of the marinade and barbecue them plain and unadorned, perhaps offering a sauce to eat with them – perfect for fussy eaters. One easy way to guarantee success is to cook all of the meat and vegetables plainly, then make a sauce or flavoured butter to be served with the food, that way children can pick and choose what they eat.

It is also a good idea to serve some non-barbecued favourites too, such as mashed potatoes, cooked pasta with butter, buns and bread rolls, baked beans or a little plain risotto. These can be enjoyed with the barbecued food, but offer a safe option for children who are not quite sure.

# chapter 3
# Meals for the Masses

A host of crowd-pleasing recipes for large numbers, which includes a planner with time-saving tips to take the stress out of catering for large parties.

# Butterflied Leg of Lamb with Flageolets

**Preparation time:** 30 minutes, plus soaking
**Cooking time:** 2 hours

Serves 6–8

250 g (8 oz, 2 cups) flageolet beans or haricot beans
2 bay leaves
large leg of lamb, boned and butterflied
3 tablespoons olive oil
4 whole garlic bulbs
25 g (1 oz, 2 tablespoons) butter
1 large onion
6 celery sticks, cut into 1 cm (½ inch) pieces
25 g (1 oz) mint or parsley leaves
crusty bread, to serve

**barbie tip**
An easy way to barbecue a whole joint like lamb is to remove the bone and flatten. This speeds up the cooking process. Or, ask your butcher to prepare the meat for you.

**1** Place the beans in a bowl with cold water to cover. Soak overnight, then drain, rinse and drain again. Tip the beans into a large saucepan, add the bay leaves and cover with cold water. Bring to the boil, boil rapidly for about 10 minutes, then lower the heat and simmer gently for 50–60 minutes until just tender. Drain the beans well, discarding the bay leaves. Set aside.

**2** Remove most of the skin and fat from the lamb, leaving only a thin layer. Brush with the oil and place flat on an oiled barbecue grill over hot coals. Sear the meat for about 5–6 minutes on each side, then turn and cook for 10–15 minutes more on each side. About 8–10 minutes before the end of the cooking time, wrap each garlic bulb in a double thickness of foil and place in the embers of the fire to soften the flesh.

**3** When the meat is cooked, transfer it to a platter, cover with a tent of foil and leave to rest for 10 minutes. Meanwhile, melt the butter in a large saucepan. Add the onion and celery and cook gently for 10–12 minutes, until softened but not coloured. Add the flageolet beans and heat through, stirring occasionally. Season to taste, remove from the heat and toss with the mint or parsley.

**4** Slice the lamb and serve with the beans. Add some roasted garlic to each portion and offer plenty of crusty bread.

# Kofta Kebabs

*This speciality from the Middle East consists of spiced minced lamb or beef pressed around skewers, grilled and served with a minty yogurt dip. Metal skewers are most authentic.*

**Preparation time:** 20 minutes
**Cooking time:** 10–12 minutes

Serves 8

1 kg (2 lb) minced lamb or beef
2 onions, grated
125 g (4 oz, 1 cup) pine nuts, toasted and chopped
2 tablespoons chopped oregano
1 teaspoon ground cumin
1 teaspoon ground coriander
salt and pepper

**barbie tip**
To toast pine nuts, place them in a dry frying pan over a medium heat and move them around continuously until they are golden brown.

YOGURT DIP:
600 ml (1 pint, 2½ cups) Greek yogurt
6 tomatoes, skinned, deseeded and chopped
2 tablespoons chopped mint
¼ teaspoon cayenne pepper

TO SERVE:
toasted pitta breads
Cos lettuce

**1** To make the dip, mix the yogurt, chopped tomatoes and mint in a bowl. Season with the cayenne and salt. Cover the bowl and place in the refrigerator until required.

**2** Place the minced lamb or beef in a blender or food processor and mix to a smooth paste. Alternatively, pass through the finest blade of a mincer. Scrape into a bowl and stir in the onion, pine nuts, oregano and spices. Season with salt and pepper.

**3** Mould the mixture around 8 long skewers, forming it into flat sausage shapes. Place the skewers on a well-oiled grill over hot coals and cook for about 10–12 minutes, turning frequently, until the meat is browned all over and cooked through.

**4** Remove the kebabs from the skewers and serve with toasted pitta breads, Cos lettuce and yogurt dip.

# Stuffed Pork Fillet

**Preparation time:** 30 minutes, plus marinating
**Cooking time:** 40–45 minutes

Serves 8

175 g (6 oz, ¾ cup) ground almonds
8 large oranges
4 tablespoons clear honey
8 tablespoons olive oil
4 tablespoons chopped oregano
1 kg (2 lb) pork fillet, trimmed
8 garlic cloves, thinly sliced
25 g (1 oz, 2 tablespoons) butter, diced
salt and pepper

**1** Spread the ground almonds on a baking sheet. Cook in a preheated oven, 180°C (350°F), Gas Mark 4, for 10 minutes until evenly golden. Remove from the oven, leave to cool, then place in a small bowl.

**2** Finely grate the rind from 4 of the oranges and add to the almonds. Add the honey to make a paste, then season to taste. Peel and segment those 4 oranges and set aside.

**3** To make the marinade, squeeze the juice from the remaining oranges into a jug. Stir in the olive oil and oregano.

**4** Slice each pork fillet lengthways, almost but not all the way through, and open it out like a book. Divide the almond mixture between the fillets. Drain the orange segments, adding any juice to the marinade. Divide the orange segments and garlic slivers between the pork fillets, arranging them on top of the almond mixture.

**5** Bring the edges of the meat together and tie the fillets with string at 2.5 cm (1 inch) intervals. Place in a shallow dish and pour over the marinade, turn to coat, cover and refrigerate for 8 hours or overnight.

**barbie tip**
Replace the oranges with 4 apples. Cut them into wedges and use to stuff the meat. Use 50 ml (2 fl oz, ¼ cup) of apple juice and 2 tablespoons of Calvados in place of the orange juice.

**6** Let the meat return to room temperature for about 1 hour then remove from the marinade. Season with salt and pepper and cook on an oiled grill over hot coals for 40–45 minutes, basting frequently with the marinade.

**7** Transfer the meat to a platter, cover with a tent of foil and leave to rest while you prepare the sauce. Tip the remaining marinade into a small saucepan and boil rapidly until reduced by half. Slowly whisk in the butter and pour into a sauceboat. Remove the string from the fillets, slice the meat and serve with the sauce.

# Sheekh Kebabs

*These kebabs are a popular street food in India. Barbecued over charcoal braziers, they are eaten with red onions, mint and hot bread.*

**Preparation time:** 10 minutes, plus chilling (optional)
**Cooking time:** 10 minutes

Makes 12

2 green chillies, deseeded and finely chopped
1 teaspoon grated fresh root ginger
2 garlic cloves, crushed
3 tablespoons chopped fresh coriander
2 tablespoons chopped mint leaves
1 teaspoon cumin seeds
1 tablespoon vegetable oil
$\frac{1}{2}$ teaspoon ground cloves
$\frac{1}{2}$ teaspoon ground cardamom seeds
500 g (1 lb) minced lamb
sea salt

**1** Put the chillies, ginger, garlic, coriander, mint, cumin, oil, ground cloves and cardamom into a food processor or blender and process until fairly smooth. Transfer to a mixing bowl, add the lamb and salt and mix well, using your hands. Divide the mixture into 12 portions, cover and chill for 30 minutes, if time allows.

**2** Lightly oil 12 flat metal skewers and shape a portion of the kebab mixture around each skewer, forming a sausage shape.

**3** Place the kebabs on an oiled rack over hot coals and cook for 3–4 minutes on each side, or until cooked through and browned.

### barbie tip
The meat mixture can also be formed into balls and threaded on to the skewers, perhaps alternating the meatballs with pieces of onion or pepper.

# Tamarind Spare Ribs with Mint Relish

Preparation time: 15 minutes, plus marinating
Cooking time: 15–20 minutes

Serves 8

2 kg (4 lb) meaty pork spare ribs

MARINADE:
2 teaspoons mustard seeds
6 tablespoons tamarind paste or 4 tablespoons lime or lemon juice
4 garlic cloves, crushed
2 tablespoons light soy sauce
12 tablespoons honey
2 teaspoons ground cumin
2 teaspoons ground coriander
1 teaspoon chilli powder

MINT RELISH:
125 g (4 oz, 2 cups) chopped mint
1 small red onion, very finely chopped
2 small green chillies, deseeded and chopped
4 tablespoons lemon juice
2 teaspoons sugar
salt and pepper

**1** To make the marinade, place the mustard seeds in a dry frying pan and cook over low heat until the seeds start to pop. Remove the pan from the heat and leave the seeds to cool, then crush them lightly.

### barbie tip
This marinade can also be used on pork or lamb chops or cutlets. The mint relish adds a sweet tanginess which contrasts well with the marinade.

**2** Mix the remaining marinade ingredients with the crushed mustard seeds. Place the spare ribs in a large shallow dish and pour over the marinade. Turn the spare ribs to coat, then cover and leave to marinate for 1–2 hours.

**3** To make the mint relish, place the mint, onion, chilli, lemon juice and sugar in a blender or food processor. Work until smooth, pushing down with a spatula occasionally. Turn out into a bowl and season to taste with salt and pepper.

**4** Remove the spare ribs from the marinade and place on an oiled barbecue grill. Cook for about 15–20 minutes, turning frequently. Serve with the mint relish.

# Chicken Tikka Kebabs with Naan

*Homemade naan bread is so delicious that it is well worth the effort of making it – especially when it is to be served with these spicy kebabs. The naan is also quite filling, so you won't have to cook so much on the barbecue to fill your guests.*

**barbie tip**
While the kebabs are cooking, wrap the naan breads in a foil parcel and heat on the edge of the barbecue grill.

**Preparation time:** 30 minutes, plus marinating
**Cooking time:** 12–15 minutes

**Serves 8**

8 naan breads (see page 158)
1.5 kg (3 lb) skinless, boneless chicken breasts, cut into 2.5 cm (1 inch) cubes
lemon or lime wedges, to garnish

MARINADE:
2 onions, roughly chopped
5 cm (2 inch) piece of fresh root ginger, peeled and roughly chopped
4 garlic cloves, crushed
300 ml (½ pint, 1¼ cups) natural yogurt
2 red chillies, deseeded and chopped
1 tablespoon ground coriander
2 teaspoons ground cumin
1 teaspoon turmeric
8 tablespoons lemon juice
2 teaspoons salt

**1** To make the marinade, combine all ingredients in a blender or food processor and purée until smooth.

**2** Place the chicken cubes in a shallow bowl, pour over the marinade and toss well to coat. Cover the bowl and leave the chicken to marinate in the refrigerator for 8 hours or overnight.

**3** Remove the chicken with a slotted spoon and pour the marinade into a jug. Thread the chicken on to 16 skewers.

**4** Cook the kebabs on an oiled barbecue grill over hot coals for 6 minutes on each side, basting frequently with the marinade. Serve the kebabs with the warm naan and garnish with wedges of lemon or lime.

# Fruit and Nut Couscous with Chicken Skewers

*This dish is inspired by the flavours of North Africa. The couscous will fill up your guests, but won't take up precious space on the barbecue.*

**Preparation time:** 20 minutes, plus marinating
**Cooking time:** 15 minutes

Serves 8

1 kg (2 lb) skinless chicken breast fillets
4 tablespoons olive oil
4 garlic cloves, crushed
1 teaspoon ground cumin
1 teaspoon ground turmeric
1 teaspoon paprika
4 teaspoons lemon juice

COUSCOUS:
8 tablespoons olive oil
2 small onions, finely chopped
2 garlic cloves, crushed
2 teaspoons each ground cumin, cinnamon, pepper
  and ginger
125 g (4 oz, ½ cup) dried dates, chopped
125 g (4 oz, ½ cup) dried apricots, finely chopped
125 g (4 oz, 1 cup) blanched almonds, toasted and
  chopped
1.2 litres (2 pints, 5 cups) vegetable stock
375 g (12 oz, 3 cups) couscous
2 tablespoons lemon juice
4 tablespoons chopped fresh coriander
salt and pepper

TO GARNISH:
seeds from half a pomegranate
lemon wedges
fresh coriander sprigs

**barbie tip**
As an alternative, make the kebabs using large prawns or pieces of vegetable. Marinate and cook in the same way. Prawns will only take 1–2 minutes on each side.

**1** Cut the chicken into long thin strips, place them in a shallow dish and add the olive oil, garlic, spices and lemon juice. Stir well, then cover and leave to marinate for 2 hours. Thread the chicken strips on to 16 small skewers.

**2** To prepare the couscous, heat half of the oil in a saucepan and fry the onion, garlic and spices for 5 minutes. Stir in the dried fruits and almonds and remove from the heat.

**3** Meanwhile, pour the stock over the couscous, cover with a tea towel and leave for 8–10 minutes, until the grains are fluffed up and the liquid absorbed. Stir in the remaining oil and the fruit and nut mixture, add the lemon juice and coriander and season with salt and pepper to taste.

**4** While the couscous is standing, cook the chicken skewers for 4–5 minutes on each side over medium coals, until charred and cooked through. Serve with the couscous, garnished with pomegranate seeds, lemon wedges and coriander sprigs.

# Cinnamon-spiced Chicken Wings

*Unusual, sweet and spicy, this is a delicious way to serve chicken wings.*

**Preparation time:** 30 minutes, plus marinating
**Cooking time:** 8–10 minutes

**Serves 8**

16 large chicken wings
fresh coriander sprigs, to garnish

MARINADE:
2 garlic cloves
8 cm (3 inch) piece of fresh root ginger, peeled and chopped
juice and finely grated rind of 4 limes or 2 lemons
4 tablespoons light soy sauce
4 tablespoons groundnut oil
4 teaspoons ground cinnamon
2 teaspoons ground turmeric
4 tablespoons honey
salt

YELLOW PEPPER DIP:
4 yellow peppers
8 tablespoons natural yogurt
2 tablespoons dark soy sauce
2 tablespoons chopped fresh coriander
pepper

**barbie tip**
Because they are quite small, you can get lots of wings on the barbie at a time, making them great for large parties.

**1** Place all the marinade ingredients in a blender or food processor and blend until very smooth. Place the chicken in a bowl, pour over the marinade, toss, cover and leave to marinate for 1–2 hours.

**2** To make the yellow pepper dip, place the yellow peppers under a preheated grill for about 10 minutes, turning until well charred and blistered all over. Place in a plastic bag until cool, then peel, deseed and place the flesh in a blender or food processor with the yogurt and blend until smooth. Pour into a bowl, add the soy sauce and season with pepper to taste; stir in the chopped coriander and set aside.

**3** Drain the chicken and cook on an oiled barbecue grill for 4–5 minutes on each side, basting with the remaining marinade. Garnish with coriander and serve with the dip.

# Whole Baked Fish in Banana Leaves

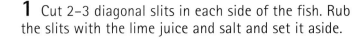

*This recipe can be made with many different sorts of fish. Try parrot fish, snapper or red sea bream.*

**Preparation time:** 20 minutes
**Cooking time:** 20–30 minutes

Serves 4

1 whole fish, about 1.5 kg (3 lb), cleaned and scaled
1 tablespoon lime juice mixed with 1 teaspoon salt
1 small onion, roughly chopped
1 red or yellow pepper, cored, deseeded and roughly chopped
2.5 cm (1 inch) piece of fresh root ginger, peeled and roughly chopped
2 garlic cloves, roughly chopped
2 fresh red chillies, deseeded and roughly chopped
1 lemon grass stalk, chopped
125 ml (4 fl oz, ½ cup) coconut milk
½ teaspoon chilli powder
15 g (½ oz, ½ cup) fresh coriander
banana leaves or kitchen foil, for wrapping

**1** Cut 2–3 diagonal slits in each side of the fish. Rub the slits with the lime juice and salt and set it aside.

**2** Place all the remaining ingredients, except the wrapping, in a blender or food processor and purée until smooth. Scrape the paste into a bowl.

**3** Dip the banana leaves, if using, into boiling water. Drain and lay the fish on top. Rub a quarter of the paste into the fish, turn the fish over and rub in another quarter of the mixture. Wrap the leaves securely around the fish, making sure that there are no holes in the parcel; tie with string. Alternatively, wrap the fish in a double thickness of foil.

**4** Place the wrapped fish on a barbecue grill over moderately hot coals. Cook for 10–15 minutes on each side, until the flesh is tender. Transfer the parcel to a large platter and turn back the leaves or foil to reveal the fish. Heat the remaining paste in a small saucepan and serve with the fish.

**barbie tip**
Scale up the quantities, depending on the number of guests you have – each fish will serve 4 guests. Cooking whole fish like this is an efficient use of barbecue space.

# Grilled Mackerel with Plum Sauce

*This pretty plum sauce is perfect with mackerel, providing a slightly acidic counterpoint to the oiliness of the fish. Mackerel are inexpensive and delicious, making them a great choice for large gatherings. They also fit closely together on the grill, meaning you can cook lots together.*

**Preparation time:** 25 minutes
**Cooking time:** 10–15 minutes

**Serves 8**

1 kg (2 lb) sharp red plums
50 g (2 oz, ¼ cup) sugar
2 teaspoons coriander seeds, crushed
2 garlic cloves, crushed
pinch of paprika
2 teaspoons finely grated lemon rind
8 tablespoons water
8 whole mackerel, about 375 g (12 oz) each
salt and pepper

**1** Cut the plums in half, remove the stones and cut the flesh into wedges. Place in a saucepan with the sugar, coriander seeds, garlic, paprika, lemon rind and water. Bring to the boil, cover, lower the heat and simmer gently for about 10 minutes, until softened.

**2** Spoon the plum mixture into a blender or food processor and purée until smooth. Sieve into a clean pan, bring to the boil and cook for 5 minutes, until thickened and reduced, stirring constantly to prevent the sauce from burning.

**3** Cut 3 diagonal slashes on both sides of each fish. Season and cook on an oiled barbecue grill over hot coals for 6–7 minutes on each side.

**4** Place the freshly grilled mackerel on individual plates. Pour the hot, thick plum sauce into a bowl or sauceboat, and serve immediately with the grilled fish.

### barbie tip
If you are not keen on serving fish on the bone, use mackerel fillets instead. Serve 2 fillets per person and cook for 3–4 minutes each side.

# Baby Aubergines with Herbed Greek Yogurt

**Preparation time:** 20 minutes
**Cooking time:** 6 minutes

Serves 8

24 baby aubergines
6 tablespoons olive oil
toasted pitta breads, to serve (optional)

HERBED GREEK YOGURT:
4 tablespoons chopped parsley
4 tablespoons chopped dill
4 tablespoons chopped mint
1 red onion, finely chopped
4 garlic cloves, crushed
150 g (5 oz, 1½ cups) Kalamata olives, pitted and sliced
4 tablespoons fennel seeds, crushed
2 tablespoons capers, chopped
25 g (1 oz, ¼ cup) gherkins, finely chopped
finely grated rind and juice of 2 limes
300 ml (½ pint, 1½ cups) strained Greek yogurt
salt and pepper

**1** To make the herbed Greek yogurt, mix all the ingredients and set aside. Make it well ahead so the flavours have time to mingle.

**2** Slice all the baby aubergines in half lengthways, leaving the aubergines attached to their stalks. Using a small brush, coat the aubergines with olive oil. Cook on an oiled barbecue grill over moderately hot coals for about 2–3 minutes on each side.

**3** To serve, place the aubergines on a serving dish or plate and spoon over the herbed yogurt.

**barbie tip**
For ease of cooking and turning, the baby aubergines can be threaded on skewers if you like.

# Get Organized

If you get yourself organized well in advance, a barbecue can be one of the easiest ways of entertaining, especially for large groups of people. And because it's always a fairly informal event, there is not so much pressure for you to perform as the perfect host and cook. It's good to be prepared in advance, though, to save time on the day and make sure you've got everything you need for a hassle-free event.

As with any party, let guests help when they offer, whether it's serving drinks, passing round nibbles, or a stint in front of the barbecue. To relieve the stress even further, provide fairly substantial nibbles with drinks so it doesn't matter how long the food takes to cook. A few plates of Bruschetta with Grilled Pepper and Hazelnuts (see page 146) or Chicken Yakitori (see page 110) will always go down well. If you are having lots of friends over, borrowing an extra barbecue will be a great help as there never seems to be quite enough cooking space. However, make sure you've got enough cooks and lots of charcoal.

## Time-saving Tips

✳ Serve a mixture of barbecued and non-barbecued dishes to save cooking time on the barbecue and ensure everyone gets fed at the same time. For example, serve jacket potatoes, lots of bread and a large selection of ready-made salads with barbecued meats. Alternatively, choose dishes like Tuna Niçoise (see page 24) which can mostly be made in advance, with just the chargrilled tuna to be barbecued and added to the salad at the last minute. Fruit and Nut Couscous with Chicken Skewers (see page 56) are also a good choice, as only the skewers need last-minute attention and everything else can be made in advance.

✳ You can ask your butcher to prepare the meat for you or buy the meat already cut into pieces, such as cubed pork, chicken drumsticks, trimmed spare ribs or individual cutlets.

✳ Ask your fishmonger to scale and gut fish, and fillet them if necessary.

✳ Cook large prawns in their shells as they retain more flavour and juiciness. Or, if you really want them unshelled, look for them ready peeled.

✳ Most marinades, sauces, herb butters and so on can be made well in advance. Some will also freeze successfully.

✳ Some butchers and supermarkets sell products ready for barbecuing, such as marinated spare ribs and chicken portions, or even kebabs complete with pieces of pepper and onion skewered with the meat. While not usually quite as nice as the homemade variety, these are perfectly acceptable if you are catering for a large party or simply don't have the time.

✳ Some foods, such as spare ribs, sausages and mackerel, take up little room on a barbecue and can be packed in close together making efficient use of what space you have. This means you can cook lots of the food in one batch and serve plenty of people at once.

✳ Some vegetables are quicker to prepare than others. For example, cherry tomatoes, button mushrooms and baby aubergines can be threaded straight on to skewers without any preparation. Or cook whole field mushrooms or sweetcorn cobs which don't need to be cut up first.

✳ For large parties, choose desserts which can be prepared in advance and served cold, such as Fresh Blueberry Cheesecake (see page 172), or even some good quality ice creams or sorbets with a selection of sweet biscuits.

* Advance preparation is the key to any meal, but it is especially important when you are catering for crowds. Most barbecue foods can be prepared up to the point of cooking the day before, if you cover them and keep them chilled. Meat can be rinsed, dried and cut up, and you can make up kebabs in advance. If you are marinating the food on the kebabs, use wooden skewers and put the kebabs, skewers and all, into the marinade overnight. (Metal skewers may react with the marinade.)

* Burger mixture and sausagemeat can be made a day or two in advance, and if you use meat that has not been previously frozen, you can make the burgers and sausages the week before and freeze them until the day of the party.

* Prepare vegetables such as peppers, courgettes, onions, potatoes and beans the day before and store them in sealed plastic bags or boxes in the refrigerator.

## Things to Remember

**One week before**
Buy charcoal
Check and refill gas bottle
Buy firelighters or twigs for kindling
Make sure you have matches
Clean the barbecue, including the grill rack
Plan the menu and drinks
Check you have serviettes
Find out guests' likes and dislikes, and how many are vegetarians
Plan seating arrangements in the garden, including shade for hot weather
Make a wet-weather plan if there's a chance it may rain.

**The day before**
Defrost frozen foods
Rinse the meat and pat dry with kitchen paper
Cut up meat and poultry into cooking portions
Prepare and cut up vegetables
Make up skewers
Marinate meat where necessary
Make herb butters
Make garlic or herb oil for basting
Make sauces and dips
Sort out cutlery, crockery, glasses and serviettes
Find serving dishes
Make or buy lots of ice for drinks

**On the day**
Prepare and light the barbecue half an hour before you plan to start cooking; fifteen minutes for gas
Work out the order of cooking before you start – decide which foods need longest and get them going first. Also decide which items will keep warm in an oven
Turn on the oven for keeping food warm, if necessary
Chill drinks
Keep meat and fish refrigerated until 1 hour before cooking, then return them to room temperature in a cool place
Make salads and accompaniments
Put out sauces, such as ketchup and mustard
Put out bread and rolls
Prepare and serve nibbles while the barbecue heats up
Accept offers of help – barbecues should be informal and fun
Pour yourself a drink and get sizzling

## Checklist

charcoal or gas
firelighters or kindling
matches
barbecue tools
apron for cook(s)
serviettes

cutlery
plates
glasses
skewers
serving plates
drinks
nibbles
meat, fish or vegetables for

barbecuing
bread, rolls or pittas
salads and other accompaniments
sauces – ketchup, mustard, mayonnaise and so on
desserts

# chapter 4
# Weekday Wind-down

Simple and delicious recipes which can be prepared in minutes for easy after-work barbecues. This chapter also features clever suggestions for using what's already in the store cupboard and freezer so that you won't have to do a special shop.

# Kidney and Bacon Skewers

*The pancetta will help baste the kidneys and prevent them from drying out, while sage gives the meat a delicious flavour.*

**Preparation time:** 15 minutes
**Cooking time:** 6–8 minutes

Serves 4

6 lambs' kidneys
6 slices of pancetta or rindless streaky bacon, halved
1 red onion, cut into wedges
1 bunch of sage, leaves stripped from the stalks
50 g (2 oz, ¼ cup) butter, melted
salt and pepper

**1** Split the kidneys in half and carefully remove the core and fat. Score the rounded side of each half kidney in a criss-cross pattern.

**2** Wrap a slice of pancetta around each piece. Thread the kidney and bacon pieces on to 4 long skewers, alternating with red onion wedges and sage leaves.

**3** Season the brochettes with salt and pepper, brush with melted butter and cook on an oiled barbecue grill over hot coals for 3–4 minutes on each side, basting frequently with the remaining butter.

**barbie tip**
When cutting the onion into wedges, take care to keep the root end intact so the leaves of the onion are held together.

# Duck Breasts with Caramelized Olives and Oranges

**Preparation time:** 15 minutes, plus salting
**Cooking time:** 25–30 minutes

Serves 4

4 duck breasts, about 250 g (8 oz) each
250 g (8 oz, 1 cup) coarse sea salt
4 oranges
2 pieces of stem ginger in syrup, drained and chopped
125 g (4 oz, 1 cup) black olives
15 g (½ oz, 1 tablespoon) butter
pepper

**barbie tip**
Salting the duck before cooking draws out any excess moisture and makes the skin crisp.

**1** Place one duck breast, skin side up, on a large double piece of foil, sprinkle with half of the salt and top with a second duck breast, skin side down. Wrap tightly in foil. Repeat with the remaining pair of duck breasts. Chill both parcels for at least 12 hours, preferably 24–36 hours.

**2** To prepare the caramelized mixture, finely grate the rind of 2 of the oranges, then peel and segment all 4, working over a bowl to catch any juices. Place the segments in the bowl and mix in the orange rind, ginger and olives. Place this mixture on a large doubled piece of foil with the edges turned up (or use an aluminium tray), and dot with the butter. Place the open parcel on an oiled barbecue and grill over hot coals for about 25–30 minutes, tossing the mixture every now and then, until the oranges are slightly caramelized.

**3** Meanwhile, separate the duck breasts, rinse them well and pat dry on kitchen paper. Season with pepper and cook on the oiled barbecue grill, skin side down, for the first 5 minutes then turn and seal the other side. Continue cooking the duck alongside the parcel of olives and oranges for 10–15 minutes, turning occasionally, until the duck skin is crisp and the flesh tender but still pink. Serve with the olive and orange mixture.

# The Great Steak Sandwich

*This sandwich, spread with a sweet onion purée and topped with succulent steak, creamy fontina cheese, tomato and peppery rocket, is a meal in itself. The onion purée can be made the day before if you are short of time.*

**Preparation time:** 15 minutes
**Cooking time:** 30 minutes

Serves 4

6 tablespoons olive oil
2 teaspoons mustard seeds
2 large red onions, thinly sliced
2 garlic cloves, crushed
15 g (½ oz, ½ cup) flat leaf parsley, chopped
1 tablespoon balsamic vinegar
2 rump or sirloin steaks, about 250 g (8 oz) each
crushed black peppercorns
8 slices of olive bread or crusty bread
75 g (3 oz) fontina cheese, thinly sliced
2 ripe beefsteak tomatoes, sliced
125 g (4 oz) rocket
sea salt and pepper

**1** Heat 4 tablespoons of the olive oil in a frying pan, add the mustard seeds, cover and let them pop for 30 seconds over moderate heat – do not let them burn. Add the onions and garlic and cook over a very low heat for 30 minutes until very soft but not coloured.

**2** Purée the softened onion mixture in a blender or food processor, then spoon into a bowl. Stir in the parsley and vinegar, with salt and pepper to taste. Cover and set aside.

**3** Brush the steaks with a little of the remaining oil. Season with crushed black peppercorns. Cook on an oiled barbecue grill over hot coals for 2–3 minutes on each side for very rare, up to 5–6 minutes each side for medium or 10–12 minutes for well done.

**4** Toast the bread slices on both sides until lightly golden. Spread with the onion purée. Slice the steaks thinly and divide between 4 of the bread slices. Top with the fontina, tomato slices and rocket. Season with salt and pepper, top with the remaining bread slices and serve at once.

## barbie tip
Don't season the steaks with salt before cooking or you will draw moisture to the surface of the steaks and prevent the meat being sealed properly.

# Spicy Asian Pork Chops

**Preparation time:** 10 minutes, plus marinating
**Cooking time:** 15–20 minutes

Serves 4

4 loin pork chops, about 250 g (8 oz) each
fresh coriander sprigs, to garnish

MARINADE:
3 garlic cloves
2 tablespoons palm or light muscovado sugar
15 black peppercorns
1 lemon grass stalk, roughly chopped
2 tablespoons Thai fish sauce
1 tablespoon Chinese rice wine
1 teaspoon sesame oil
2 tablespoons groundnut oil

**1** First make the marinade. Put the garlic, sugar, peppercorns, lemon grass, fish sauce, rice wine, sesame oil and groundnut oil into a small food processor and work to a paste. If you prefer, you can pound the first 4 ingredients to a paste in a mortar and add the next 4 ingredients to the paste, little by little, as you pound it. Mix it all thoroughly.

**2** Place the pork chops in a shallow dish and cover them completely with the marinade. Cover the dish and leave to marinate in the refrigerator overnight.

**3** Transfer the chops to a grill rack and cook over medium coals for about 8 minutes on each side, until lightly browned and cooked through. Serve the chops garnished with coriander sprigs.

**barbie tip**
Don't put the chops too close to the coals or the outsides will burn before the insides are cooked through.

# Thai Barbecued Chicken

*This delicious chicken can be spatchcocked and put into the marinade the night before, so it just needs to be cooked when you come home after a busy day at work.*

**Preparation time:** 20 minutes, plus marinating
**Cooking time:** 30–40 minutes

**Serves 4–6**

5 cm (2 inch) piece of fresh galangal or ginger, peeled and finely chopped
4 garlic cloves, crushed
1 large red chilli, finely chopped
4 shallots, finely chopped
2 tablespoons finely chopped fresh coriander leaves
150 ml (¼ pint, ⅔ cup) thick coconut milk
1.5 kg (3 lb) chicken, spatchcocked (see page 10)
salt and pepper

TO SERVE:
sweet chilli sauce, for dipping
lime wedges

**1** Put the galangal or ginger, garlic, red chilli, shallots and coriander in a food processor and blend to a paste or use a pestle and mortar. Add the coconut milk and mix until well blended.

**2** Rub the chicken all over with salt and pepper and place in a shallow container. Pour the coconut marinade over the chicken, cover and leave to marinate overnight in the refrigerator.

**3** Remove the chicken from the marinade, place it on a hot barbecue and cook for 30–40 minutes, turning and basting regularly with the remaining marinade. The whole chicken is cooked when a skewer inserted in one of the legs reveals clear juices.

**4** Leave the chicken to stand for 5 minutes, then chop it into small pieces. Serve with sweet chilli dipping sauce and lime wedges.

**barbie tip**
Chicken portions, such as part-boned chicken breasts or thighs, can be used instead of a whole chicken but only cook them for 10–15 minutes.

# Pesto Turkey Kebabs

**barbie tip**
Adjust the distance between the grill rack and the coals as necessary while you cook to make sure they are lightly browned on the outside and cooked right through.

**Preparation time:** 15 minutes
**Cooking time:** about 12 minutes

Serves 4

4 turkey breast steaks, about 500 g (1 lb) in total
2 tablespoons Pesto (see page 120)
8 slices of Parma ham
125 g (4 oz, ½ cup) sundried tomatoes in oil, drained and finely chopped
125 g (4 oz) mozzarella cheese, finely diced
1 tablespoon olive oil
salt and pepper
chopped parsley, to garnish
lemon wedges, to serve

**1** Place a turkey steak between 2 sheets of clingfilm and pound it lightly with a mallet until it is about 1 cm (½ inch) thick. Repeat with the remaining steaks.

**2** Spread pesto over each thinned turkey steak and lay 2 slices of Parma ham on top of each. Sprinkle the tomatoes and mozzarella evenly over the turkey steaks, then season to taste and roll up each one from the long side.

**3** Cut the turkey rolls into 2.5 cm (1 inch) slices. Carefully thread the slices of roll on to 4 metal skewers, dividing them equally among the skewers.

**4** Brush the turkey rolls lightly with oil and barbecue over medium coals for 6 minutes on each side or until cooked through. Garnish with chopped parsley and serve hot, with lemon wedges.

# Mediterranean Prawns

*Tiger prawns are delicious, if expensive, making this simple dish an absolute delight. It is very quick to prepare, so there should be no problem cooking this for friends after work.*

**Preparation time:** 10 minutes, plus marinating
**Cooking time:** 4–6 minutes

Serves 4

500 g (1 lb) raw tiger prawns, in their shells
4 tablespoons olive oil
2 garlic cloves, finely crushed
1 teaspoon ground cumin
$\frac{1}{2}$ teaspoon ground ginger
1 teaspoon paprika
$\frac{1}{4}$ teaspoon cayenne pepper
bunch of coriander, finely chopped
salt
lemon wedges, to serve

**1** Peel and devein most of the prawns, leaving a few whole since they look so attractive.

**2** Mix the olive oil, garlic, cumin, ginger, paprika, cayenne pepper and coriander in a bowl. Add the prawns and toss to combine. Season with salt and leave to marinate while you light the barbecue.

**3** Divide the prawns between four skewers. Cook them for 2–3 minutes on each side over medium coals. Serve hot, accompanied by lemon wedges.

### barbie tip
These prawns can also be butterflied for a more exotic effect. Peel the prawns and use scissors to cut them lengthways almost in half, leaving the tails intact.

# Seafood Brochettes with Saffron Mayonnaise

*Monkfish and sweet scallops, lightly chargrilled outside and soft and tender inside, are served with a creamy golden mayonnaise. Make the mayonnaise the day before if you like.*

**Preparation time:** 25 minutes, plus marinating
**Cooking time:** 3–4 minutes

Serves 4

375 g (12 oz) monkfish fillet, skinned and cut into
    2.5 cm (1 inch) cubes
12 scallops, cut in half crossways if large

MARINADE:
2 teaspoons lime juice
3 tablespoons sunflower oil
salt and pepper

SAFFRON MAYONNAISE:
pinch of saffron threads
1 tablespoon boiling water
2 egg yolks
1 tablespoon lemon juice
200 ml (7 fl oz, 1 scant cup) sunflower oil

**1** First prepare the saffron mayonnaise. Place the saffron threads in a small bowl. Pour over the boiling water and leave to infuse for 10 minutes. Combine the egg yolks and lemon juice in a separate bowl. Add the saffron and its soaking liquid and whisk the mixture until slightly thickened. Continue to whisk briskly, gradually adding the oil in a thin stream until the mixture forms a thick, creamy mayonnaise. Taste and adjust the seasoning.

**2** Mix the marinade ingredients together in a jug. Place the cubes of monkfish and the prepared scallops in a shallow dish, then pour the marinade over the fish and set aside in the refrigerator while you light the barbecue.

**3** When you are ready to cook, use a slotted spoon to remove the fish from the marinade. Thread alternate pieces of fish and scallops on 8 skewers. Return the marinade to the jug.

**4** Cook the brochettes on an oiled barbecue grill over moderately hot coals for about 3–4 minutes, turning frequently and basting with the remaining marinade. Serve immediately with the saffron mayonnaise.

### barbie tip
Many types of seafood could be used in these kebabs. Try chunks of cod, salmon, swordfish or tuna, or large peeled prawns or pieces of squid instead.

# Chargrilled Mustard Salmon with Lime Courgettes

**Preparation time:** 5 minutes
**Cooking time:** 10–15 minutes

Serves 4

4 salmon fillets, about 200 g (7 oz) each
1 tablespoon prepared English mustard
1 teaspoon grated fresh root ginger
1 teaspoon crushed garlic
2 teaspoons clear honey
1 tablespoon light soy sauce

LIME COURGETTES:
2 tablespoons olive oil
500 g (1 lb) courgettes, thinly sliced lengthways
grated rind and juice of 1 lime
2 tablespoons chopped mint
salt and pepper

**1** Place the salmon fillets, skin side down, in a shallow flameproof dish. They should fit snugly in a single layer. Mix the mustard, ginger, garlic, honey and soy sauce, then spoon this mixture evenly over the fillets. Season to taste and set aside.

**2** To prepare the lime courgettes, heat the olive oil in a large nonstick frying pan. Add the courgettes and fry, stirring often, for 5–6 minutes or until they are lightly browned and tender. Stir in the lime juice and rind, mint and seasoning. Remove from the heat and keep hot.

**3** While the courgettes are cooking, place the salmon fillets on the barbecue and cook for 10–15 minutes, depending on their thickness, until lightly charred and cooked through. Serve hot with the lime courgettes.

**barbie tip**
If you have space, cook the courgettes alongside the salmon. Brush the courgette slices with oil and cook for 2–3 minutes on each side, then drizzle with the lime juice and rind, mint and seasoning.

# Swordfish with Toasted Almond and Parsley Pesto

**Preparation time:** 10 minutes
**Cooking time:** 10 minutes

Serves 4

125 g (4 oz, 1 cup) unblanched whole almonds
1 garlic clove, crushed
2 tablespoons finely grated Parmesan cheese
50 g (2 oz, 2 cups) parsley, roughly chopped
200 ml (7 fl oz, 1 scant cup) extra virgin olive oil
2 tablespoons fresh ricotta cheese
4 swordfish steaks, about 175 g (6 oz) each
olive oil, for brushing
salt and pepper
lemon wedges, to garnish

**1** Spread the almonds on a baking sheet and place it under a preheated grill for 2–3 minutes, turning the almonds often until they are toasted and golden. (You may have to break one open to see.)

**2** Place half of the toasted almonds in a blender or food processor with the garlic, Parmesan, parsley, olive oil, ricotta and salt and pepper and blend until smooth, scraping down the sides of the bowl if necessary. Roughly chop the remaining almonds and stir into the pesto.

**3** Brush the swordfish steaks with olive oil and cook over hot coals for 2–3 minutes on each side or until just cooked through. Season with salt and pepper and serve the fish with the pesto, garnished with lemon wedges.

**barbie tip**
Serve this herb and nut pesto with any barbecued fish. You can also vary the flavours by using basil or coriander instead of the parsley.

# Swordfish with Mustard and Chive Butter

**Preparation time:** 5 minutes, plus chilling
**Cooking time:** 6–8 minutes

Serves 4

100 g (3½ oz, ½ cup) butter, softened
2 tablespoons finely snipped chives
1 tablespoon prepared English mustard
4 swordfish steaks or fillets, about 200 g (7 oz) each
4 tablespoons lemon juice
salt and pepper

To GARNISH:
whole chives
lemon wedges

To SERVE:
cherry tomato salad
boiled rice or new potatoes

**1** In a small bowl, mix the butter, chives and mustard. Turn the butter out on to a piece of greaseproof paper and press it out into a sausage shape. Wrap the paper around the butter, twist the ends and roll the butter into a neat sausage, then chill it in the freezer for 10–15 minutes or until firm.

**2** Lay the swordfish on a grill rack over hot coals and sprinkle with lemon juice. Season the fish well and grill for 6–8 minutes or until cooked through, when the fish will flake easily.

**3** While the fish is grilling, remove the butter from the freezer and cut it into slices. Transfer the fish to warmed serving plates and top with the butter. Garnish with chives and lemon wedges and serve at once. A cherry tomato salad and boiled rice or new potatoes go well with the fish.

**barbie tip**
Mahi mahi and halibut are particularly good in place of the swordfish as they are also firm and flavoursome.

# Impromptu Barbecues

It's nice to light up the barbecue when the mood takes you, perhaps when the weather is particularly fine or a few friends drop round unexpectedly. Barbecued meals don't have to be huge and you don't have to have several different sorts of meat every time – just enjoy the simple pleasure of cooking outside.

## Move it Outside

It's usually possible to adapt whatever you were planning to have for dinner anyway, as most ingredients can be barbecued. For example, Pork Chops with Apple Sauce and Parsnips (see page 40) can be cooked on the barbecue, or you could make burgers out of the fish you were planning to have for dinner – see Fish Burgers with Yogurt Mayo (see page 41). If you had bought minced beef to make spaghetti bolognese, why not make Kofta Kebabs (see page 50) instead?

## Using your Imagination

With a little imagination, it's usually possible to make a meal out of what you've got in the storecupboard or freezer. Plain cuts of meat and most vegetables can be barbecued as they are, then transformed with a sauce or herb butter. Try Mixed Herb Butter (see page 184) or Salmoriglio Sauce (see page 184); both are simple to make and don't require any unusual ingredients.

If you have a recipe in mind but find you are missing one of the ingredients, in most cases it can be simply left out. Making barbecue food is not like baking cakes – the recipe won't fail just because you don't have 2 teaspoons of light soy sauce. You could also swap it for something else – for example substitute lemon juice for lime juice, light soy sauce for Thai fish sauce, parsley for mint, thyme for rosemary and so on.

## Vegetables

Vegetables are great barbecue staples and if you don't have a large and varied assortment of meats in the house, you will probably have a good selection of vegetables. Plenty of vegetables are suitable for barbecuing and they can make up a large part of the meal. For ideas, see pages 140–1. Either barbecue the vegetables as they are, or make simple skewers, such as Mediterranean Kebabs (see page 43). Hasselback Potatoes (see page 94) are another great staple – all you need are some potatoes, olive oil, sea salt and a sharp knife.

## Frozen Meat and Fish

The freezer is the first place to start looking when you decide on the spur of the moment that you want a barbecue. It's a good idea to keep a supply of basic barbecue foods in your freezer.

✳ Choose smaller cuts of meat which will defrost quickly and won't take up too much space on the barbecue, such as sausages, chops and chicken thighs.

✳ Fish steaks and large raw prawns are another delicious standby.

✳ Freeze meat and fish in small packages, perhaps with just two portions in each one, so they will defrost quickly and you can get out just the right amount for the number of people eating.

✳ Use a microwave to defrost frozen foods quickly, or seal them in a plastic bag and place it in a bowl of cold water to speed up the process.

## Storecupboard Ingredients

olive oil
cumin seeds
fennel seeds
ground coriander
chilli powder
black peppercorns
soy sauce
Thai fish sauce
white wine vinegar
mustard
coconut cream

## Store in the Refrigerator

haloumi cheese
feta cheese
peppers
courgettes
mushrooms
onions
lemons
garlic
fresh root ginger
herbs
salad ingredients

## Store in the Freezer

sausages
minced beef or lamb
pork steaks and chops
lamb chops
chicken portions
spare ribs
bag of large raw prawns
tuna or swordfish steaks
chillies

## Quick and Easy Recipes

Lemon and Herb Chicken Wings (see pages 30–1)
Barbecued Potato Wedges with Sundried Tomato Aioli
  (see page 42)
Mediterranean Kebabs (see page 43)
Kofta Kebabs (see page 50)
Mediterranean Prawns (see page 73)
Sweetcorn with Skorthalia (see page 136)

Feta and Cherry Tomato Kebabs (see page 132)
Spicy Burgers (see page 18)
Peppered Chicken Skewers with Rosemary
  (see page 21)
Grilled Sardines with Chilli Oil (see page 22–3)
Potato Skins with Soured Cream (see page 27)
Coconut Butterfly Prawns (see page 25)

# chapter 5
# Elegant Entertaining

Barbecues don't have to be casual affairs –
entertain in style and treat your guests to
sumptuous chargrilled food on special occasions.

# Balsamic Figs Grilled with Prosciutto

*This is an easy and quick starter to cook on the barbecue. The balsamic vinegar caramelizes on the figs, giving a sweet and sour flavour.*

**Preparation time:** 10 minutes
**Cooking time:** 5 minutes

Serves 4

8 fresh ripe figs
2 tablespoons balsamic vinegar
2 tablespoons extra virgin olive oil, plus extra to serve
12 slices of prosciutto

TO SERVE:
Parmesan cheese shavings
crushed black pepper

**1** Take the figs one at a time and stand them upright. Using a sharp knife, make 2 cuts through each fig, not quite quartering them but keeping them intact. Ease the figs open and brush with the balsamic vinegar and olive oil.

**2** Place the figs, cut side down, on the barbecue and cook for 3–4 minutes until hot and slightly charred.

**3** While the figs are cooking, place half of the slices of prosciutto on the barbecue and cook until frazzled and starting to crisp. Remove and keep warm while cooking the remaining prosciutto.

**4** To serve, arrange 3 pieces of prosciutto and 2 figs each on 4 warmed plates. Cover with Parmesan shavings, drizzle with a little more olive oil and sprinkle with plenty of crushed black pepper.

**barbie tip**
If you can't get fresh figs, peaches will do just as well. Halve and stone the peaches and cook them cut side down on the barbecue in the same way.

# Venison with Red Juniper Pears

*Pears in red wine, usually seen as a dessert, are also wonderful with rich venison.*

**Preparation time:** 20 minutes, plus cooling
**Cooking time:** 25 minutes

Serves 4

4 firm dessert pears
2 tablespoons lemon juice
300 ml (½ pint, 1¼ cups) red wine
6 juniper berries, crushed
pared rind of 1 lemon, cut into fine julienne strips
1 cinnamon stick
3 tablespoons redcurrant jelly
8 venison cutlets
oil or melted butter, for brushing
watercress, to garnish

**Barbie tip**

These pears can also be served with other full-flavoured barbecued meats, such as pork, pheasant or guinea fowl.

**1** Peel the pears, then halve them lengthways and remove the cores with a teaspoon. Brush the flesh with the lemon juice to prevent the pears from discolouring.

**2** Combine the wine, juniper berries, lemon rind and cinnamon stick in a saucepan. Bring to the boil, add the pears, cover and simmer gently for 10 minutes or until tender.

**3** Using a slotted spoon, transfer the pears to a bowl and set aside. Stir the redcurrant jelly into the liquid remaining in the pan. Boil until reduced by half, pour over the pears and leave to cool.

**4** Brush the venison cutlets with a little oil or butter. Cook on an oiled barbecue grill over hot coals for 2–3 minutes on each side. To serve, place 2 cutlets on each plate and add a portion of pears. Garnish with watercress and serve the remaining pears separately.

# Calves' Liver and Prosciutto Kebabs with Onion Relish

**Preparation time:** 15 minutes
**Cooking time:** 5–6 minutes

Serves 4

375 g (12 oz) calves' liver, sliced and skinned
6–8 slices of prosciutto
2 tablespoons thyme leaves
16 bay leaves
2 tablespoons olive oil
salt and pepper
Onion Relish, to serve

**1** Cut the calves' liver and prosciutto into 7 x 2.5 cm (3 x 1 inch) slices. Place a strip of prosciutto on each piece of liver, then sprinkle with a little thyme and season with salt and pepper.

**2** Roll up from the short end and thread on to a skewer. Repeat with the remaining calves' liver and prosciutto until all the skewers have been filled, adding bay leaves at regular intervals. Brush the kebabs with the olive oil.

**3** Cook the kebabs on an oiled barbecue grill over hot coals for about 5–6 minutes, turning frequently. Serve at once with onion relish.

### barbie tip
Calves' liver should be cooked quickly so it is tender and juicy in the middle and browned on the outside.

## Onion Relish

**Preparation time:** 15 minutes
**Cooking time:** 40 minutes

Serves 4

50 g (2 oz, ¼ cup) butter
4 large red onions, sliced
2 tablespoons thyme leaves
1 tablespoon red wine vinegar
1 tablespoon caster sugar

**1** First melt the butter in a large frying pan. Stir in the onions and thyme and cover the pan. Cook the onions gently for 40 minutes, until softened but not coloured, stirring once.

**2** Remove the lid and stir in the vinegar and sugar, then increase the heat and boil rapidly to reduce the juices. Spoon into a bowl and serve warm or cold.

# Guinea Fowl with Mushroom Stuffing

*The guinea fowl is spatchcocked for ease of cooking, and stuffed under the skin with a mushroom mixture which keeps the flesh moist during grilling.*

**Preparation time:** 20 minutes, plus soaking
**Cooking time:** 40–50 minutes

Serves 4

1–1.5 kg (2–3 lb) guinea fowl, spatchcocked (see page 10)
butter or oil, for brushing

MUSHROOM STUFFING:
25 g (1 oz) dried porcini mushrooms, soaked in warm water for
   30 minutes
50 g (2 oz, ¼ cup) butter
2 shallots, finely chopped
1 garlic clove, crushed
250 g (8 oz) field mushrooms, finely chopped
2 tablespoons chopped parsley
salt and pepper

**1** To make the stuffing, drain the porcini through a sieve lined with kitchen paper or a coffee filter paper. Reserve the liquid and finely chop the mushrooms.

**2** Melt the butter in a saucepan. Add the shallots and garlic and cook gently for 2–3 minutes, until softened but not coloured. Add both types of mushrooms and cook for 4–5 minutes more. Stir in the reserved mushroom liquid and boil hard until all the liquid has evaporated. Off the heat, stir in the parsley and add salt and pepper to taste. Cool slightly.

**3** Gently lift and loosen the skin of the guinea fowl, easing it away from the breast and leg meat with your fingers. Take care not to make any holes. Spoon the stuffing under the skin and spread it out evenly. Pull the skin back tightly over the bird and secure underneath with a skewer or cocktail sticks.

**4** Brush the guinea fowl with a little butter or oil. Cook breast side down on an oiled barbecue grill over hot coals for 10–15 minutes. Turn the bird over and cook for 10–15 minutes more. Continue cooking, turning occasionally, until the juices run clear when the thickest part of a thigh is pierced with a fork or skewer.

**5** Transfer the guinea fowl to a platter, cover with a tent of foil and keep warm until ready to carve.

### barbie tip
Barbecued apple wedges or rings are particularly good with this guinea fowl. Brush the apple pieces with butter and cook for 1–2 minutes on each side.

# Partridges with Port and Grape Sauce

**Preparation time:** 15 minutes
**Cooking time:** 25 minutes

Serves 4

4 oven-ready partridges, about 375 g (12 oz) each
1 onion, quartered
4 strips of lemon rind
4 slices of pancetta or rindless streaky bacon, halved lengthways
50 g (2 oz, ¼ cup) butter, slightly softened
1 tablespoon chopped parsley
4 tablespoons brandy, warmed in a ladle
salt and pepper

SAUCE:
6 juniper berries, crushed
50 ml (2 fl oz, ¼ cup) port
3 tablespoons redcurrant jelly
500 g (1 lb) black grapes, cut in half lengthways and deseeded

**1** Stuff each partridge with an onion quarter and a strip of lemon rind. Place 2 strips of pancetta across the breast of each one and tie with string. Mix the butter, parsley, salt and pepper, and spread some over each bird.

**2** Place a drip tray on the hot coals of a barbecue and place an oiled grill rack on the setting nearest the coals. Sear the birds for 2–3 minutes on each side. Raise the rack to a position 10–12 cm (4–5 inches) from the coals. Cook the partridges for 12–15 minutes more, turning frequently, until the birds are tender and the juices run clear when the thickest part of the thigh is pierced.

**3** Transfer the birds to a heated platter, ignite the ladle of warmed brandy and pour over. Make a tent of foil over the birds to keep them hot.

**barbie tip**
Other game birds can be cooked in the same way. Try pheasants, pigeons, squabs and quails, adjusting the cooking time accordingly.

**4** Pour the juices from the drip tray into a saucepan. Add the juniper berries, port, redcurrant jelly and the grapes. Bring to the boil, reduce for 2–3 minutes, skim the surface, then pour the sauce into a bowl. Serve with the partridges.

# Pink Pigeon Breast Salad

*A pretty salad of warm pigeon breasts with pink peppercorns, pomegranate and raspberries – a stunning starter for a smart barbecue party.*

**Preparation time:** 20 minutes, plus marinating
**Cooking time:** 10 minutes

Serves 4

1 pomegranate
2 shallots, chopped
1 teaspoon pink peppercorns bottled in brine, drained
   and crushed
8 wood pigeon breasts
1 tablespoon sugar
125 g (4 oz, 1 cup) raspberries, hulled
melted butter, for brushing
1 radicchio, separated into leaves
1 bunch of watercress or rocket
50 g (2 oz, ½ cup) walnuts, chopped

**1** Break open the pomegranate and remove the seeds, discarding the bitter yellow pith. Set aside a quarter of the seeds for the sauce and place the rest in a blender or food processor. Process just long enough to release the juice, then strain through a fine sieve into a shallow bowl. Add the shallots and pink peppercorns. Mix well, then add the pigeon breasts and toss to coat. Cover the dish and marinate for 1–2 hours.

**barbie tip**
Some people are allergic to pink peppercorns, so you may wish to substitute with crushed black or white ones.

**2** Using a slotted spoon, lift the pigeon breasts out of the marinade and set aside. Pour the marinade into a saucepan, stir in the sugar, bring to the boil and cook until reduced by half. Add the raspberries and reserved pomegranate seeds, remove from the heat immediately and set the sauce aside while you cook the pigeon breasts.

**3** Brush the pigeon breasts with a little melted butter. Place on an oiled barbecue grill over hot coals and sear quickly on both sides for 1–2 minutes. Remove the breasts from the heat and slice thinly.

**4** Arrange the radicchio and watercress or rocket on 4 plates. Top with the pigeon breasts, spoon over the sauce and sprinkle with the chopped walnuts. Serve at once.

# Scallop and Monkfish Skewers with Fennel Sauce

**Preparation time:** 15 minutes, plus marinating
**Cooking time:** 5–6 minutes

Serves 4
4 dried fennel stalks, about 20 cm (8 inches) long
500 g (1 lb) monkfish fillets
8 large scallops
2 tablespoons olive oil
1 garlic clove, crushed
salt and pepper
bread, to serve

FENNEL SAUCE:
3 tablespoons chopped fennel or dill
pinch of dried chilli flakes
2 teaspoons lemon juice
6–8 tablespoons olive oil
1 fennel bulb

### barbie tip
Dried fennel stalks make good skewers as they are rigid and impart flavour into the food during cooking. Rosemary stems can be used in the same way.

**1** Pull off the dried leaves still attached to the fennel stalks, leaving a clump at one end, and soak the stalks in cold water for at least 30 minutes.

**2** Cut the monkfish into 12 large chunks about the same size as the scallops and place in a ceramic dish. Cut away the tough white muscle from each scallop and remove any intestine. Wash and pat dry and add to the monkfish.

**3** Stir in the olive oil, garlic and some pepper until the seafood is thoroughly coated; cover and marinate for at least 30 minutes. Thread the pieces of seafood on to the herb stalks.

**4** Meanwhile, make the fennel sauce. Mix together the fennel or dill, chilli flakes, lemon juice and oil, and season with salt and pepper to taste. Cover and set aside to infuse. Just before serving, thinly slice the fennel bulb and toss with the sauce.

**5** Season the seafood with salt and cook over hot coals for 5–6 minutes, turning the skewers halfway through and basting with the marinade, until charred and tender. Serve the skewers hot, with the fennel sauce and some bread to mop up the juices.

# Barbecued Squid and Prawns

*When barbecued, the flavour of squid and fresh prawns can be fully appreciated – this cooking method gives a smoky, sweet, chargrilled taste, a perfect complement to the hot peppery sauce.*

**Preparation time:** 20 minutes, plus marinating
**Cooking time:** 25 minutes

Serves 4

375 g (12 oz) prepared squid
12 large raw prawns in their shells

RED PEPPER SAUCE:

2 red peppers
2 red chillies
1 tablespoon sherry vinegar
salt and pepper

MARINADE:

3 tablespoons chopped oregano
5 tablespoons olive oil
2 shallots, finely chopped
1 tablespoon lemon juice

**1** To prepare the sauce, place the peppers and chillies under a hot, preheated grill. Cook the peppers for 10–15 minutes and the chillies for 5–6 minutes, turning occasionally. When their skins are well charred and blistered, transfer the chillies and peppers to a polythene bag, close the top lightly and set aside to cool.

**2** Rub off the charred skin, then cut the peppers and chillies in half and remove and discard the seeds. Pat the vegetables dry with kitchen paper, then place them in a blender or food processor. Add the sherry vinegar and blend until smooth. Add salt and pepper to taste.

**3** Cut the squid flesh into 2.5 cm (1 inch) squares and score the squares in a criss-cross pattern. Place the squid and prawns in a shallow dish. Mix the marinade ingredients in a jug, then pour the mixture over the seafood. Toss to coat, then cover and marinate for 30–40 minutes.

**4** Using a slotted spoon, remove the seafood from the marinade, then pour the marinade into a jug. Thread the squid and prawns on to wood or metal skewers.

**5** Cook the brochettes on an oiled barbecue grill over moderately hot coals for 6–8 minutes, turning once and basting frequently with the remaining marinade. Place the brochettes in deep soup bowls and pour the sauce over the top.

**barbie tip**
Don't forget that if you are using wooden skewers, soak them in cold water for about 30 minutes before adding the seafood.

# Salmon and Samphire en Papillote

*Samphire – or sea asparagus as it is also known – is a delicious coastal plant which grows on salt marshes. Here it is combined with rich salmon and a nutty pistachio and basil butter in a foil parcel. You probably won't need to add any salt as the samphire is already quite salty.*

**Preparation time:** 15 minutes
**Cooking time:** 15-20 minutes

Serves 4

4 salmon fillets, about 200 g (7 oz) each
150 g (5 oz) samphire
Hasselback Potatoes, to serve

PISTACHIO AND BASIL BUTTER:
125 g (4 oz, ½ cup) butter, slightly softened
50 g (2 oz, ½ cup) shelled, unpeeled, unsalted pistachio nuts
2 tablespoons chopped basil
1 garlic clove, crushed
1–2 teaspoons lime juice
salt and pepper

**1** To make the pistachio and basil butter, place the butter, pistachios, basil, garlic and lime juice in a blender or food processor. Add salt and pepper to taste and blend until the sauce is smooth and green. Spoon the mixture into a small bowl, cover and chill in the refrigerator.

**2** Place each salmon fillet on a double piece of foil large enough to enclose it completely. Top each fillet with a quarter of the samphire and add a generous tablespoon of the pistachio and basil butter. Bring up the edges of the foil and press together to seal each parcel.

**3** Cook the salmon parcels for 15–20 minutes over medium coals. Just before serving, carefully open one of the parcels and check the fish is cooked. It should flake easily when tested with the a knife, but still be moist. Serve the parcels with Hasselback potatoes (see right).

## Hasselback Potatoes

Preparation time: 5 minutes
Cooking time: 20–25 minutes

Serves 4

16 small new potatoes
3 tablespoons olive oil
sea salt flakes

**1** Divide the potatoes between 4 skewers. Using a small sharp knife, make thin slashes across each potato, then brush all the potatoes with the olive oil and sprinkle with some sea salt flakes.

**2** Cook the potato skewers on an oiled barbecue grill over hot coals for 20–25 minutes.

# Sea Bass with Lime Aioli

**Preparation time:** 15 minutes
**Cooking time:** 10 minutes

Serves 4

4 large potatoes, unpeeled
4 tablespoons olive oil
4 sea bass fillets, about 200 g (7 oz) each
salt and pepper

LIME AIOLI:
4–6 garlic cloves, crushed
2 egg yolks
juice and finely grated rind of 2 limes
300 ml (½ pint, 1¼ cups) extra virgin olive oil

**1** First make the aioli. Place the garlic and egg yolks in a food processor or blender, add the lime juice and process briefly to mix. With the machine running, gradually add the olive oil in a thin steady stream until the mixture forms a thick cream. Turn into a bowl, stir in the lime rind and season to taste. Set aside.

**2** Slice the potatoes thinly and brush well with olive oil. Sprinkle the slices with salt and pepper and place on a barbecue grill and cook for 2–3 minutes on each side or until tender and golden. Remove from the heat and keep warm while you cook the fish.

**3** Score the sea bass fillets, brush well with the remaining olive oil and place on the barbecue grill, skin side down. Cook for 3–4 minutes until just cooked, turning once. Remove from the heat and serve with the potatoes and the aioli.

### barbie tip
Allow the sea bass skin to cook until it is crisp before turning over the fillets. The crispy skin is delicious to eat.

# Monkfish with Garlic and Rosemary

**Preparation time:** 20 minutes, plus marinating
**Cooking time:** 15–20 minutes

Serves 4

500 g (1 lb) ripe tomatoes, skinned
1 tablespoon balsamic vinegar
2 monkfish fillets, about 375 g (12 oz) each, skinned
4 garlic cloves, cut into thin slivers
2 long rosemary sprigs
5 tablespoons olive oil
1 tablespoon lemon juice
salt and pepper
crusty bread, to serve

**1** Place the tomatoes in a blender or food processor and purée until smooth. Strain through a sieve into a bowl, season to taste with the vinegar, salt and pepper, then cover and set aside.

**2** Slice each monkfish fillet lengthways, almost but not quite all the way through, making a pocket. Lay the garlic slivers down the length of the pocket in each fillet and top with a rosemary sprig. Add salt and pepper to taste. Reform both fillets and tie them with string at 1.5 cm (¾ inch) intervals.

**3** Mix the olive oil and lemon juice in a shallow dish, large enough to hold both fillets. Add the monkfish, spoon the oil and lemon juice over the top, then cover. Marinate for 1 hour, turning occasionally.

**4** Drain the monkfish and cook on an oiled barbecue grill over moderately hot coals for 15–20 minutes, basting frequently, until the flesh is opaque and just cooked. Meanwhile, pour the tomato sauce into a small saucepan and heat through. Remove the string and slice the fish thinly. Serve with the tomato sauce and good crusty bread.

### barbie tip
Rosemary is a very powerful herb. Here the monkfish fillets are tied together with rosemary sprigs, so the aroma permeates the fish without being overwhelming.

# Tuna with Anchovies and Caper Vinaigrette

Preparation time: 15 minutes
Cooking time: 6–8 minutes

Serves 4

4 thick tuna steaks, about 250 g (8 oz) each
12 anchovies in oil, drained and cut in half
4 garlic cloves, cut into thin slivers
2 tablespoons olive oil
salt and pepper
crisp green salad, to serve

**barbie tip**
Tuna should be only just cooked or it becomes tough. If you like your tuna rare, cook the steaks for just 2 minutes on each side.

CAPER VINAIGRETTE:
100 ml (3½ fl oz, ½ cup) extra virgin olive oil
2 tablespoons white wine vinegar
1 teaspoon Dijon mustard
1 tablespoon chopped tarragon
1 tablespoon chopped flat leaf parsley
2 tablespoons capers, rinsed and drained
pinch of sugar

**1** To make the caper vinaigrette, whisk together the olive oil, vinegar and mustard in a small bowl. Stir in the tarragon, parsley and capers and season with salt, pepper and a pinch of sugar. Cover and set aside.

**2** With a small sharp knife, make 6 small incisions in each tuna steak. Using the end of the knife, poke a piece of anchovy fillet and a sliver of garlic into each incision.

**3** Brush all the steaks with olive oil and season with salt and pepper. Place the steaks on the barbecue grill and cook for 3–4 minutes on each side until just cooked. Serve with the caper vinaigrette and a crisp green salad.

# Goats' Cheese in Vine Leaves

*Goats' cheese is delicious when wrapped and grilled in vine leaves. Choose small whole cheeses such as crottins.*

**Preparation time:** 10 minutes
**Cooking time:** 8 minutes

Serves 4

4–8 vine leaves, fresh or preserved in brine
1 tablespoon chopped thyme leaves
1 tablespoon chopped flat leaf parsley
1 tablespoon chopped oregano
1 teaspoon crushed mixed peppercorns
1 tablespoon lemon juice
4 small whole goats' cheeses
2 tablespoons olive oil

**1** If you are using vine leaves preserved in brine, rinse them well in a colander under cold running water. Bring a small saucepan of water to the boil, add the vine leaves and blanch for 1 minute. If using fresh vine leaves, remove any tough stems and blanch briefly in boiling water for 30 seconds. Regardless of type, refresh the blanched leaves under cold water, then drain well.

**2** Mix the chopped fresh herbs with the crushed peppercorns and lemon juice in a shallow bowl. Brush the goats' cheeses with olive oil and roll them in the herb mixture. Wrap the coated cheeses in the vine leaves, then brush them with any remaining olive oil.

**3** Place the wrapped goats' cheeses on an oiled barbecue grill over moderately hot coals. Cook for 8 minutes, turning once, until the cheeses are just soft.

### barbie tip
Serve with toasted crusty bread and a few salad leaves as a starter, or serve on a bed of salad as part of a buffet meal.

# Menu Planner

These are some suggested menus for different occasions, whether it's a lazy afternoon barbie, or sophisticated dinner. It's easy enough to double up quantities for the recipes if you have a lot of guests, or reduce them accordingly for smaller parties. The dishes in each menu offer a balanced meal, but of course you can swap one or two of the recipes for something else if you prefer. If you want a themed barbecue, there are more menu suggestions on pages 120–1.

**Brunch for the Masses**
Kidney and Bacon Skewers (see page 66)
Spicy Burgers (see page 18)
Homemade Sausages with Mustard Aioli (see page 16)
Fish Burgers with Yogurt Mayo (see page 41)
Grilled Haloumi Wrapped in Radicchio (see page 129)
Potato Skins with Soured Cream (see page 27)
hotdog buns
tomato ketchup
Spiced Coleslaw (see page 151)
Fresh green salad
Figs and Blackberries on Toast (see pages 168–9)
Coffee Meringues (see page 175)
Raspberry Sorbet (see page 178)

**Intimate Dinner**
Goats' Cheese in Vine Leaves (see page 99)
toasted crusty bread
Monkfish with Garlic and Rosemary (see pages 96–7)
Grilled Sweet Potato and Aioli (see page 160)
Green Salad with a Mixed Herb Sauce (see page 156)
Tiramisu with Raspberry Surprise (see pages 176–7)
cheese and biscuits

**Lazy Afternoon**
Tandoori Chicken (see page 20)
Barbecued Squid and Prawns (see page 93)
Grilled Sardines with Chilli Oil (see page 22)
Watercress and Pomegranate Salad (see page 153)
Tomato and Green Bean Salad (see pages 154–5)
crusty bread
Fresh Blueberry Cheesecake (see pages 172–3)

**Sunshine Lunch**
Chicken on Lemon Grass Skewers (see pages 112–3)
Tuna Niçoise (see page 24)
Seafood Brochettes with Saffron Mayonnaise (see page 74)
Mediterranean Kebabs (see page 43)
Cucumber, Radish and Dill Salad (see page 152)
Olive, Caper and Sundried Tomato Focaccia (see pages 148–9)
Raspberry Sorbet (see page 178)

**Barbecue to Impress**
Bruschetta with Grilled Pepper and Hazelnuts (see page 146)
Goats' Cheese in Vine Leaves (see page 99)
Butterflied Leg of Lamb with Flageolets (see pages 48–9)
Whole Baked Fish in Banana Leaves (see page 59)
boiled new potatoes
baby leaf salad with Mint Dressing (see page 188)
Chocolate and Praline Truffle Terrine (see page 174)
Champagne Syllabub with Strawberries (see page 179)

## Large Party

Tamarind Spare Ribs with Mint Relish (see page 54)
Homemade Sausages with Mustard Aioli (see page 16)
Chicken Tikka Kebabs with Naan (see page 55)
Grilled Mackerel with Plum Sauce (see page 60)
Baby Aubergines with Herbed Greek Yogurt (see page 61)
Sweetcorn with Skorthalia (see page 136)
Tabbouleh and Fennel Salad (see page 159)
Orecchiette, Broad Bean and Pecorino Salad (see page 158)
Greek Country Salad (see page 157)
Fresh Blueberry Cheesecake (see pages 172–3)
good quality ice cream

## Special Occasion

Olives Marinated with Asian Flavours (see page 145)
Balsamic Figs Grilled with Prosciutto (see pages 84–5)
Calves Liver and Prosciutto Kebabs with Onion Relish (see page 87)
Chicken Yakitori (see page 110)
Stuffed Pork Fillet (see page 51)
Pink Pigeon Breast Salad (see pages 90–1)
Nut Koftas with Minted Yogurt (see pages 130–1)
Asparagus with Balsamic Tomato Dressing (see page 134)
Orecchiette, Broad Bean and Pecorino Salad (see page 158)
Watercress and Pomegranate Salad (see page 153)
Champagne Syllabub with Strawberries (see page 179)

## Informal Family Meal

Lemon and Herb Chicken Wings (see pages 30–1)
Lamb Cutlets with Rosemary and Lemon (see page 38)
Feta and Cherry Tomato Kebabs (see page 132)
boiled new potatoes
Spiced Coleslaw (see page 151)
Bananas with Mascarpone and Rum Cream (see page 164)

## Fuss-free Fun

Spicy Burgers (see page 18)
Lemon and Herb Chicken Wings (see pages 30–1)
Mediterranean Prawns (see page 73)
Aubergine Steaks with Miso (see page 124)
boiled new potatoes
green salad with Classic Vinaigrette (see page 188)
strawberries and cream

## Kids' Party

Turkey, Tomato and Tarragon Burgers (see page 34)
Lemon and Herb Chicken Wings (see pages 30–1)
Homemade Sausages with Mustard Aioli (see page 16)
Potato Skins with Soured Cream (see page 27)
baked beans
hotdog buns
tomato ketchup
cucumber and tomato chunks
ice cream

## Barbecue Bonanza

Spare Ribs with Ginger (see page 37)
The Great Steak Sandwich (see page 68–9)
Chicken Satay (see page 32)
Spicy Burgers (see page 18)
Fish Burgers with Yogurt Mayo (see page 41)
Mediterranean Kebabs (see page 43)
Spiced Coleslaw (see page 151)
Tiramisu with Raspberry Surprise (see pages 176–7)

# chapter 6

# East-West

Give your barbecue an exotic twist with these mouthwatering recipes inspired by specialities from around the world. This chapter also features ideas for throwing a themed barbecue, from Mediterranean to East-West fusion.

# Grilled Lemon Grass Beef

**Preparation time:** 10 minutes, plus marinating
**Cooking time:** 6 minutes

Serves 4

4 lemon grass stalks, finely chopped
4 large shallots, finely chopped
2 small red chillies, finely chopped
3 large garlic cloves, finely chopped
1 teaspoon salt
1 teaspoon pepper
1 tablespoon groundnut oil
750 g (1½ lb) lean rump steak, cut into 1 cm (½ inch) cubes

To serve:
herb salad
Dipping Sauce
French bread

**1** Put the lemon grass, shallots, chillies, garlic, salt, pepper and oil in a mortar and pound together, or process in a small food processor. Mix well with the beef, cover and marinate at room temperature for at least 3 hours.

**2** Thread the beef cubes on to presoaked bamboo skewers. Cook over hot coals for about 3 minutes on each side, turning occasionally. Serve with the salad, dipping sauce and pieces of French bread.

## Dipping Sauce

**Preparation time:** 2 minutes

Serves 4

3 tablespoons white wine or Chinese rice wine vinegar
3 tablespoons dark soy sauce
1½ teaspoons caster sugar
2 small red chillies, finely sliced

**1** Combine all the ingredients in a bowl and stir until the sugar has dissolved.

**barbie tip**
This recipe also works wonderfully well with chicken or pork. Use the same quantity of meat and cut into even cubes.

# Hanoi Grilled Pork

**Preparation time:** 20 minutes, plus standing
**Cooking time:** 10 minutes

Serves 4

1 tablespoon light muscovado sugar
2 tablespoons Thai fish sauce
1 large garlic clove, finely chopped
1 large shallot, finely chopped
2 teaspoons palm or golden caster sugar
1 teaspoon salt
500 g (1 lb) boneless pork loin, minced
250 g (8 oz) rice noodles, cooked
lettuce leaves, torn
125 g (4 oz) bean sprouts
handful of coriander, basil leaves, mint leaves and chives
Dipping Sauce (see page 90), to serve

**1** Gently melt the light muscovado sugar with two-thirds of the fish sauce in a heavy-based saucepan, stirring all the time. Allow to cool a little then transfer it to a bowl and combine it with the garlic, shallot, palm or caster sugar, the remaining fish sauce and salt. Add the minced pork, mix thoroughly, then cover and leave to stand for 3 hours.

**2** Shape the minced pork into 20–24 flat little patties, about 2.5 cm (1 inch) in diameter, then cook over medium-hot coals for 3–4 minutes on each side.

**3** To serve, divide the noodles between 4 warmed bowls, add the pork, torn lettuce leaves, bean sprouts and herbs. Spoon the dipping sauce over everything.

### barbie tip
Make sure the patties are cooked right through – pork should never be served raw. If you are unsure, break one in half and look at the middle.

# Satay Lembu

*These barbecued skewers are full of the aromatic flavour of Malayan cooking.*

**Preparation time:** 10 minutes, plus marinating
**Cooking time:** 6–8 minutes

Serves 4

300 ml (½ pint, 1¼ cups) coconut milk
2 garlic cloves, crushed
pinch of ground cardamom
pinch of ground cinnamon
pinch of ground cumin
pinch of curry powder
2 teaspoons fresh root ginger, chopped
freshly ground black pepper
625 g (1¼ lb) rump steak, cut into 5 cm
    (2 inch) cubes
Spicy Peanut Sauce (see page 185), to serve

To garnish:
lime wedges
mint sprigs

**1** Pour the coconut milk into a container. Add the garlic, cardamom, cinnamon, cumin, curry powder, ginger and black pepper. Stir well to combine, then stir in the steak cubes. Mix well and leave to marinate in the refrigerator for 4–6 hours.

**2** Thread the meat on to presoaked bamboo skewers or long metal skewers. Drain well and cook over hot coals for 3–4 minutes on each side. Serve garnished with lime wedges and mint sprigs, accompanied by spicy peanut sauce.

### barbie tip
These ingredients will also serve 8 as a starter. Cut the meat into 2.5 cm (1 inch) pieces and thread on to 8 skewers. Cook for just 2–3 minutes on each side.

# Jamaican Jerk Chicken

*Jerk pork is one of Jamaica's most famous national dishes. It is cooked over hot coals at roadside stands all over the island. Here, chicken drumsticks are 'jerked' instead of pork, making them perfect outdoor food to eat with your fingers.*

**barbie tip**

Jerk seasoning can be used with other cuts of chicken, such as thighs or breasts. It is also very good with pork.

**Preparation time:** 15 minutes, plus marinating
**Cooking time:** about 20 minutes

Serves 4–6

2 tablespoons rapeseed oil
1 small onion, finely chopped
10 allspice berries
2 hot red chillies, deseeded and roughly chopped
3 tablespoons lime juice
1 teaspoon salt
12 chicken drumsticks

**1** Put all of the ingredients, except the chicken drumsticks, in a food processor or spice mill and grind to a paste.

**2** Score the chicken drumsticks deeply with a sharp pointed knife, cutting right down as far as the bone.

**3** Coat the chicken with the jerk seasoning mixture, brushing it into the slashes in the meat so that the flavour will penetrate. Cover and marinate in the refrigerator overnight.

**4** Place the drumsticks on a grill rack over hot coals. Cook, turning frequently, for about 20 minutes until the chicken is charred on the outside and no longer pink on the inside. Serve hot, warm or cold.

# Chicken Teriyaki with Soba Noodles

*The combination of hot grilled chicken and cold noodles is exquisite.*

**Preparation time:** 10 minutes, plus marinating
**Cooking time:** 4–6 minutes

Serves 4

4 skinless chicken breast fillets
4 tablespoons dark soy sauce, plus extra to serve
4 tablespoons mirin
2 tablespoons caster sugar
250 g (8 oz) soba noodles
sesame oil, to serve

**1** Cut the chicken breasts into 2.5 cm (1 inch) cubes and place in a shallow dish. Combine the soy sauce, mirin and sugar, add to the chicken and toss well to coat. Set aside to marinate for 15 minutes.

**2** Meanwhile, cook the noodles according to the packet instructions, then drain, refresh in iced water, drain again and chill.

**3** Thread the chicken cubes on to metal skewers and barbecue or grill for 2–3 minutes on each side. Toss the noodles with a little sesame oil and serve with the chicken and extra sesame oil and soy sauce.

**barbie tip**
Try Salmon Teriyaki instead. Use 4 salmon fillets instead of the chicken, and cook them whole for 2–3 minutes on each side until only just cooked.

# Chicken Yakitori

*Small morsels of chicken meat and chicken livers are grilled until almost tender, then dipped in a sweet sticky glaze and returned to the grill to finish cooking.*

**Preparation time:** 15 minutes
**Cooking time:** 5–6 minutes

Serves 4

250 g (8 oz) chicken livers, cut into 1.5 cm (¾ inch) pieces
4 skinless chicken thighs, cut into 5 x 1 cm (2 x ½ inch) strips
1 green pepper, cored, deseeded and cut into 1.5 cm (¾ inch) squares
6 spring onions, cut into 1.5 cm (¾ inch) lengths
pepper

BASTING SAUCE:
4 tablespoons sake
4 tablespoons dark soy sauce
2 tablespoons light soy sauce
2 tablespoons sugar

TO SERVE:
grated white mouli (radish)
sliced cucumber

**1** To make the basting sauce, place the sake, the soy sauces and the sugar in a small saucepan, bring to the boil, remove from the heat and set aside to cool.

**2** Thread the chicken livers on to 8 presoaked bamboo skewers and chicken meat on to another 8, adding alternate pieces of green pepper and spring onion to both. Sprinkle with pepper.

**3** Cook the skewers on an oiled barbecue grill over moderately hot coals for 3 minutes, then remove from the grill and brush well with the basting sauce. Return to the grill and continue to cook, basting frequently with the remaining sauce, until tender. The chicken thigh meat will take a total of 5–6 minutes and the chicken livers 4–5 minutes.

**4** Serve immediately, with grated mouli and sliced cucumber.

### barbie tip

These small tasty skewers – the ultimate Japanese fast food – are perfect appetizers to serve with beer at a barbecue lunch or dinner party.

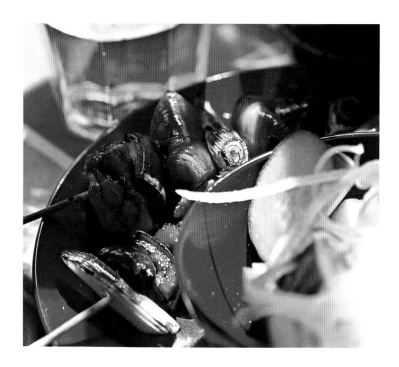

# Honey and Orange Chicken Sticks with Toasted Corn Salsa

**Preparation time:** 20 minutes, plus marinating
**Cooking time:** 20 minutes

Serves 4

2.5 cm (1 inch) piece of fresh root ginger, peeled and very finely grated
2 garlic cloves, crushed
finely grated rind and juice of 1 orange
2 tablespoons olive oil
2 tablespoons honey
4 boneless chicken breasts
green salad, to serve

TOASTED CORN SALSA:
2 corn cobs, husks and inner silks removed
3 tablespoons sunflower oil
4 spring onions, chopped
3 tablespoons chopped fresh coriander
2 teaspoons toasted sesame seeds
1 tablespoon lime juice
1 tablespoon light soy sauce
1 teaspoon sesame oil
salt and pepper

**1** First make the marinade. Place the ginger, garlic, orange rind and juice, oil and honey in a large bowl and mix together. Cut each chicken breast into 8 long thin strips and coat thoroughly with the marinade. Cover and leave to marinate for 1–2 hours.

**2** To make the toasted corn salsa, brush the corn cobs with 2 tablespoons of the sunflower oil and place under a preheated grill. Cook for 10–15 minutes, turning frequently, until the cobs are charred and the kernels are tender. Remove from the heat and, when cool enough to handle, remove the kernels from the cobs with a knife.

**barbie tip**
The corn cobs can be cooked on the barbecue rather than under a grill if it is convenient.

**3** Place the kernels in a bowl, add the remaining oil, the spring onions, coriander, sesame seeds, lime juice, soy sauce and sesame oil and season to taste. Set aside.

**4** Remove the chicken strips from the marinade and thread on skewers, 2 pieces to each skewer. Place the skewers on the barbecue grill and cook for 2–3 minutes on each side until cooked through, basting with any remaining marinade. Serve with the toasted corn salsa and a green salad.

# Chicken on Lemon Grass Skewers

**Preparation time:** 15 minutes
**Cooking time:** 10–12 minutes

Serves 4

300 g (10 oz) minced chicken
1 garlic clove, crushed
1 teaspoon grated fresh root ginger
1 tablespoon Thai fish sauce
2 teaspoons ground cumin
2 teaspoons ground coriander
1 tablespoon finely chopped coriander
1 red chilli, deseeded and finely chopped
1 teaspoon sugar
grated rind and juice of 1 lime
1 tablespoon desiccated coconut
8 lemon grass stalks
salt and pepper

TO SERVE:
boiled rice
mixed salad

**1** Put all the ingredients except the lemon grass in a bowl. Season well, then use your hands to pound and press the mixture together until thoroughly blended. Cover and chill for 10 minutes.

**2** When you are ready to cook the skewers, divide the chicken mixture into 8 equal-sized portions. Mould a portion of mixture on to the end of a lemon grass stalk, forming a sausage shape. Repeat with the remaining portions of mixture and lemon grass.

**3** Cook over very hot coals for 5–6 minutes on each side or until the chicken mixture is cooked through. Serve hot, with boiled rice and a mixed salad.

**barbie tip**
The flavour of the lemon grass is released as the skewers cook, infusing an incredible perfume and subtle spice into the chicken.

# Sizzling Fish in Banana Leaves

*This delicious Vietnamese dish can also be made with large king prawns or chicken fillets instead of the fish.*

**Preparation time:** 20 minutes
**Cooking time:** 8–10 minutes

**Serves 4**

4 large squares of banana leaf
4 swordfish, snapper or sea bass fillets, 2.5 cm
   (1 inch) thick
salt and pepper

SPICE PASTE:
1 lemon grass stalk, very finely chopped
2 large garlic cloves, finely chopped
1 kaffir lime leaf, finely shredded
2 shallots, finely chopped
125 g (4 oz, ½ cup) butter
2 teaspoons lime juice
1 tablespoon finely chopped coriander
1 green chilli, finely chopped
1 red chilli, finely chopped

**1** For the spice paste, blend the lemon grass, garlic, lime leaf and shallots to a smooth paste in a food processor or with a pestle and mortar. Add the butter, lime juice, coriander, chillies, salt and pepper and blend again.

**2** Put the banana leaves into a bowl and pour boiling water over them, then drain; this makes them easier to bend and wrap. Place a fish fillet in the centre of each leaf and cover it with some of the lemon grass mixture. Wrap it tightly and secure with a presoaked bamboo skewer or cocktail stick.

**3** Chill the fish parcels until needed or put them straight on a preheated barbecue and cook for 8–10 minutes, turning once. Serve the fish wrapped in the banana leaves. Cut open the parcel and serve immediately.

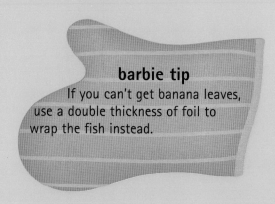

**barbie tip**
If you can't get banana leaves, use a double thickness of foil to wrap the fish instead.

# Tahini Tuna with Soba Noodles and Pak Choi

**Preparation time:** 10 minutes
**Cooking time:** 10 minutes

Serves 4

4 tuna steaks
1 tablespoon olive oil
4 tablespoons tahini paste
250 g (8 oz) soba noodles
4 baby pak choi
6 tablespoons soy sauce
4 tablespoons rice wine vinegar
2 teaspoons clear honey
1 teaspoon sesame seeds, toasted
sea salt and pepper
lemon or lime wedges, to serve

**1** Season the tuna steaks with salt and coarsely ground pepper and coat with olive oil. Cook over hot coals for 3–4 minutes on one side. Carefully turn the tuna steaks over and spread the top of each steak with some of the tahini paste. Cook for a further 3–4 minutes.

**2** Meanwhile, bring a saucepan of water to the boil, add the soba noodles and pak choi and simmer for 5 minutes or until the noodles are just cooked.

**3** Mix the soy sauce, rice wine vinegar and honey. Drain the noodles and pak choi and pour the soy mixture over them both and toss together. Put a mound of noodles on each plate and top with the tuna and pak choi. Sprinkle with the toasted sesame seeds and serve with lemon or lime wedges.

**barbie tip**
To toast sesame seeds, place them in a dry frying pan and cook, stirring frequently, until they are golden.

# Prawn and Mango Kebabs

**Preparation time:** 10 minutes, plus marinating
**Cooking time:** 4–5 minutes

Serves 4

16 large raw tiger prawns, peeled and deveined
1 tablespoon sunflower oil
4 tablespoons lemon juice
2 garlic cloves, crushed
1 teaspoon grated fresh root ginger
1 teaspoon chilli powder
1 tablespoon honey
1 teaspoon sea salt
1 large mango, peeled, pitted and cut into 8 bite-sized
   pieces
dressed salad, to serve

**1** Put the prawns in a large bowl and add the oil, lemon juice, garlic, ginger, chilli powder, honey and salt. Mix well and marinate for about 10 minutes.

**2** Remove the prawns from the marinade and thread 2 prawns alternately between 2 pieces of mango on each of 8 skewers.

**3** Place the skewers on a grill rack over hot coals, brush with the remaining marinade, and grill for 2 minutes on each side, or until the prawns turn pink and are cooked through. Serve 2 skewers on each plate, with some dressed salad.

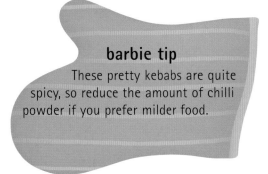

**barbie tip**
These pretty kebabs are quite spicy, so reduce the amount of chilli powder if you prefer milder food.

# Seared Peppered Tuna

**Preparation time:** 20 minutes, plus marinating
**Cooking time:** 2 minutes

Serves 4

250 g (8 oz) rice noodles
1½ tablespoons sesame oil
1½ tablespoons sesame seeds, toasted, plus 1 tablespoon
 for garnish
2 tablespoons lime juice
5 tablespoons groundnut oil
2 garlic cloves, crushed
4 tuna steaks, skinned
4 tablespoons dried pink peppercorns, crushed
salt
Pickled Ginger, to serve

**1** Prepare the noodles according to the packet instructions. Drain and refresh under cold water, then drain well again. Tip the noodles into a bowl, add the sesame oil and sesame seeds and toss lightly.

**2** Combine the lime juice, groundnut oil, garlic and salt to taste in a shallow dish, large enough to hold all the tuna in a single layer. Add the fish, toss lightly until coated, cover the dish and marinate the tuna for 1 hour, turning once.

**3** Place the peppercorns on a plate. Drain the tuna, discarding the marinade. Roll the edges of each tuna steak in the peppercorns. Sprinkle with a little salt.

**4** Cook on an oiled barbecue grill over moderately hot coals for 1 minute on each side to sear the edges. Slice thinly and serve with the ginger and noodles, sprinkled with sesame seeds to garnish.

## Pickled Ginger

**Preparation time:** 5 minutes
**Cooking time:** 2 minutes

Serves 4

6 tablespoons rice vinegar
1 tablespoon sugar
1 teaspoon salt
50 g (2 oz, about 2 inches) piece of fresh root ginger, peeled and
 cut into wafer-thin slices

**1** To prepare the pickled ginger, place the rice vinegar, sugar and salt in a small saucepan. Bring to the boil, add the sliced ginger, lower the heat and simmer for about 1–2 minutes. Remove from the heat, transfer to a bowl and leave to cool.

# Spiced Pumpkin Wedges with Coconut Pesto

*Creamy coconut pesto makes a perfect foil to the soft, nutty wedges of barbecued pumpkin dusted with curry spices.*

**Preparation time:** 15 minutes
**Cooking time:** 12–16 minutes

Serves 4

1 kg (2 lb) pumpkin
1 teaspoon cumin seeds
1 teaspoon coriander seeds
2 cardamom pods
3 tablespoons sunflower oil
1 teaspoon caster sugar or mango chutney

COCONUT PESTO:
25 g (1 oz, 1 cup) coriander leaves
1 garlic clove, crushed
1 green chilli, deseeded and chopped
pinch of sugar
1 tablespoon shelled pistachio nuts, roughly chopped
6 tablespoons coconut cream
1 tablespoon lime juice
salt and pepper

**barbie tip**
Leave the skin on the wedges as it stays firm and makes cooking and turning the pumpkin much easier.

**1** Cut the pumpkin into thin wedges about 1 cm (½ inch) thick and place in a large dish. Dry-fry the whole spices until browned, then grind to a powder in a spice grinder. Mix with the oil and sugar or mango chutney and toss with the pumpkin wedges to coat.

**2** Cook the wedges over hot coals for 6–8 minutes on each side, until charred and tender.

**3** Meanwhile, make the pesto. Put the coriander leaves, garlic, chilli, sugar and nuts into a food processor. Process until fairly finely ground and blended. Season to taste with salt and pepper. Add the coconut cream and lime juice and process again. Transfer to a serving bowl and serve with the pumpkin wedges.

# Themed Barbecues

These menu suggestions are for barbecues with different themes, from Classic Italian to Sumptuous Seafood. All lend themselves to entertaining, and it can be good fun to continue the theme to include the drinks, crockery, cutlery and seating arrangements. For more menu suggestions, see pages 100–1.

## Big Easy BBQ

This selection would suit a children's cowboy themed party. Use red-and-white checked linen and hay-bales for seating, but keep them away from the barbie. Beer or classic American cocktails would be appropriate drinks.
**Why not try:**
Homemade Sausages with Mustard Aioli (see page 16), Spicy Burgers (see page 18), Spare Ribs with Ginger (see page 37), Potato Skins with Soured Cream (see page 27) and Spiced Coleslaw (see page 151). Don't forget the ketchup and pickles. Finish with a classic, such as Fresh Blueberry Cheesecake (see page 172).

## Sumptuous Seafood

A desert island theme would be perfect. Blues and sea-greens would be ideal for crockery and linen, and you could decorate the table with shells, coconuts and driftwood. Try rum punch or rum-based cocktails.
**Why not try:**
Mediterranean Prawns (see page 73), Sea Bass with Lime Aioli (see page 95), Scallop and Monkfish Skewers with Fennel Sauce (see page 92). You could accompany this with Orecchiette, Broad Bean and Pecorino Salad (see page 158) and a tomato and red onion salad and conclude with Chocolate and Praline Truffle Terrine (see page 174).

## Mediterranean Sunshine

Mediterranean food is about strong flavours and colours: use bold-coloured crockery and use woody herbs such as rosemary to decorate napkins and as kebab skewers. Sangria goes with most Mediterranean cuisines.
**Why not try:**
Bruschetta with Grilled Pepper and Hazelnuts (see page 146) and Goats' Cheese in Vine Leaves (see page 99) to start, Lamb Cutlets with Rosemary and Lemon (see page 38), Grilled Sardines with Chilli Oil (see page 22), Greek Country Salad (see page 157) and finish with Grilled Honeyed Peaches (see page 167).

## Classic Italian

Good Italian food is based on rustic dishes, so a simple style is best. Bowls of citrus fruit, grapes and olives will not only look good, but your guests will want to enjoy them as well. Use linen with a simple stripe or check.
**Why not try:**
Grissini (see page 144) to nibble on, Balsamic Figs Grilled with Prosciutto (see page 84), Calves Liver and Prosciutto Kebabs with Onion Relish (see page 87), Monkfish with Garlic and Rosemary (see pages 96–7) and Flageolet Bean and Roasted Vegetable Salad (see page 161) to accompany. Finish your themed meal with an Italian classic with a twist, such as Tiramisu with Raspberry Surprise (see page 176–7).

## Japanese Theme

Serve your Japanese barbecue on a low table with guests seated on cushions, and use rice bowls and chopsticks to continue the theme. Drink green tea and saki to stay in theme.
**Why not try:**
Chicken Yakitori (see page 110), Tahini Tuna with Soba Noodles and Pak Choy (see page 116), salmon fillets with Teriyaki Marinade (see page 182), Aubergine Steaks with Miso (see page 124) and finish with Rum-flambéed Pineapple Parcels (see page 170).

## Vietnamese Feast

Bright-coloured paper lanterns hung in the trees will give an oriental feel, as will napkins made of satiny fabric in bold-colours and small patterns. Decorate the table with bowls of exotic flowers and floating candles.
**Why not try:**
cucumber batons with Spicy Peanut Sauce (see page 185) for dipping, Grilled Lemon Grass Beef (see page 104), Hanoi Grilled Pork (see page 105), Coconut Butterfly Prawns (see page 25) and finish with an exotic fruit platter.

## East-West Fusion

Vibrant-coloured linen would complement the colours of the food, as would terracotta-coloured candle-holders and lanterns. Decorate the table and napkins with typical herbs, such as lemon grass and lime leaves.
**Why not try:**
Satay Lembu (see page 106), Tamarind Spare Ribs with Mint Relish (see page 54), Thai Barbecued Chicken (see page 71), Spiced Pumpkin Wedges with Coconut Pesto (see page 119) and accompany with a leaf salad with Soy Sauce Dressing (see page 189). Finish with Bananas with Mascarpone and Rum Cream (see page 164).

## Asian Flavours

This wide-ranging theme gives you lots of choice: Chinese paper dragons or banners, or little Buddhas would work. Sprinkle the table with star anise or cinnamon sticks and use raffia place-mats.
**Why not try:**
Olives Marinated with Asian Flavours (see page 145) to be served as nibbles. Then move on to Chicken Satay (see page 32), Spicy Asian Pork Chops (see page 70), Chicken on Lemon Grass Skewers (see pages 112–3), Whole Baked Fish in Banana Leaves (see page 59) and finish with Barbecued Fruits with Palm Sugar (see pages 165).

## Indian Aromas

Indian cooking is all about blending spices, so hot, spicy colours will work well. Spread big floor cushions around for people to sit on. As you serve, decorate the plates with sprigs of coriander. Use spicy-scented candles.
**Why not try:**
classics such as Sheekh Kebabs (see pages 52–3) and Tandoori Chicken (see page 20), and Prawn and Mango Kebabs (see page 117). Accompany with boiled basmati rice, natural yogurt, shredded iceberg lettuce and onion. Finish with cooling fresh mango and melon.

## Middle Eastern

Metallic lanterns with patterns of holes give an Arabian feel. Use floor cushions and hang fabric on the walls. Decorate the table with bowls of citrus fruits, and olive leaves and use rustic-looking pottery.
**Why not try:**
Kofta Kebabs (see page 50), Fruit and Nut Couscous with Chicken Skewers (see pages 56–7), Baby Aubergines with Herbed Greek Yogurt (see page 61), Stuffed Mini Peppers with Tomato Sauce (see page 126). Accompany with Watercress and Pomegranate Salad (see page 153). Serve with refreshing mint tea and almond biscuits.

# chapter 7

# Viva Vegetarian

These sizzling meat-free recipes will ensure vegetarians aren't left out of the fun. This chapter shows you how to barbecue a spectacular range of fruit and vegetables to keep vegetarian food exciting.

# Aubergine Steaks with Miso

**Preparation time:** 5 minutes, plus marinating
**Cooking time:** 4–8 minutes

Serves 2–4

2 aubergines
1 tablespoon groundnut oil
1 tablespoon dark soy sauce, plus extra to serve
1 tablespoon balsamic vinegar
1 tablespoon wholegrain barley miso
1 teaspoon stem ginger syrup (from a jar)
green salad sprinkled with sesame seeds, to serve

**1** Cut the aubergines lengthways into 5 mm (¼ inch) thick slices. Combine the oil, soy sauce, vinegar, miso and ginger syrup and brush all over the aubergines. Set aside to marinate for 15 minutes.

**2** Barbecue the aubergines over medium coals, basting frequently with the marinade, for 2–4 minutes on each side, until charred and tender. Serve the aubergines with a little extra soy sauce for dipping and accompanied by a green salad sprinkled with sesame seeds.

**barbie tip**
Try using 5 courgettes in place of the aubergines, cutting them into slices of the same thickness.

# Red Bean and Rice Patties

**Preparation time:** 20 minutes, plus soaking
**Cooking time:** 1 hour 20 minutes

Serves 4

125 g (4 oz, 1 cup) red kidney beans
125 g (4 oz, ½ cup) brown rice
1 tablespoon groundnut oil
1 onion, finely chopped
1 garlic clove, crushed
1 green chilli, deseeded and finely chopped
1 teaspoon cumin seeds
1 teaspoon ground coriander
½ teaspoon ground turmeric
2 eggs, beaten
lime wedges, to garnish

SAUCE:
3 tablespoons chopped coriander
25 g (1 oz, ¼ cup) pistachio nuts, chopped
2 green chillies, deseeded and finely chopped
125 ml (4 fl oz, ½ cup) Greek yogurt

**1** Place the beans in a bowl, cover with cold water and leave to soak overnight. Drain, rinse in a colander under cold running water and drain again. Place the beans in a saucepan, cover with fresh water and boil vigorously for 10 minutes. Lower the heat and simmer for 50–60 minutes, until tender. Drain, set aside to cool, then mash until smooth.

**2** Meanwhile, bring a small pan of lightly salted water to the boil, add the rice, lower the heat and simmer for about 20–25 minutes until the grains are just cooked. Drain, refresh under cold running water, then drain well.

**3** Heat the oil in a small frying pan, add the onion, garlic and chilli and cook for 5 minutes without browning the onion. Add the cumin seeds, coriander and turmeric and cook for about 1–2 minutes more, then add the contents of the frying pan to the mashed beans. Stir in the rice and mix together well. Add the eggs, and salt and pepper to taste, then mix well to combine.

**4** For the sauce, purée the coriander, pistachios and chillies in a blender or food processor until smooth. Transfer to a bowl, stir in the yogurt and season to taste.

**5** Divide the bean and rice mixture into 4 equal portions and shape into flat rounds. Brush each round with a little oil, then place on a well-oiled barbecue grill and cook over moderately hot coals for 4–5 minutes, then turn them over and cook for a further 4–5 minutes. Serve with the sauce, and garnish with lime wedges.

**barbie tip**
Make sure a crisp crust has formed on the under side of the patties before you try to turn them over and cook the other side

# Baby Brioche Florentine with Hollandaise Sauce

**Preparation time:** 15 minutes
**Cooking time:** 30–40 minutes

Serves 4

25 g (1 oz, 2 tablespoons) butter
250 g (8 oz) young leaf spinach
grated nutmeg
8 baby brioche rolls
8 quails' eggs

HOLLANDAISE SAUCE:
175 g (6 oz, ¾ cup) butter
3 egg yolks
2 tablespoons water
1 tablespoon lemon juice
salt and pepper

**1** Melt the butter in a large saucepan. Wash the spinach and add it to the pan with only the water that clings to the leaves. Cover the pan and cook for about 3–4 minutes, stirring once, until the spinach has just wilted. Drain well and transfer to a bowl. Add salt and plenty of nutmeg and pepper to taste.

**2** Cut a neat slice off the top of each brioche roll. Set the 'lids' aside, then remove sufficient crumb from the centre of each roll to create a hollow. Place a spoonful of spinach in each hollow and carefully crack a quail's egg over the top. Replace the brioche lids. Wrap each roll in a double thickness of foil and place right side up on a barbecue grill. Cook for 30–40 minutes until the eggs are just set.

**3** To make the hollandaise sauce, first melt the butter in a small pan over a low heat. Cool slightly. Mix the egg yolks and water in a large heatproof bowl. Set this over a large saucepan of barely simmering water. Whisk until light, creamy and pale in colour.

**4** Using a ladle, gradually add the melted butter in a thin stream, whisking continuously and avoiding the white milky residue at the bottom of the pan. Continue whisking until the mixture forms a thick, foamy sauce. Remove from the heat and season to taste with lemon juice, salt and pepper. Serve the sauce with the brioche.

### barbie tip

These make a great addition to a breakfast or brunch barbecue. If you are short of time, buy ready-made hollandaise sauce but it won't be quite as delicious as your own.

# Peppers and Goats' Cheese with Grilled Chilli Relish

**Preparation time:** 10 minutes
**Cooking time:** 30 minutes

Serves 4

2 red peppers
2 yellow peppers
2 individual goats' cheeses
1 tablespoon thyme leaves
2 tablespoons extra virgin olive oil
25 g (1 oz, ¼ cup) pitted black olives, finely chopped
cracked black pepper

CHILLI RELISH:
6 large red chillies
2 tablespoons lime juice
2 garlic cloves, crushed
3 tablespoons chopped flat leaf parsley or coriander
sea salt

**1** First make the chilli relish. Put the chillies on to a baking sheet and place under a preheated grill. Leave to cook for about 5–10 minutes, turning occasionally until well charred and blistered all over. Place the chillies in a plastic bag and tie the top; leave to cool. When cool enough to handle, remove the stalks and skin, cut the chillies in half and remove the seeds. Roughly chop the flesh, retaining the flavourful juices.

**2** Place the chillies in a mortar and pound with a pestle. Stir in the remaining ingredients and season with salt. Set aside.

**barbie tip**
Try using 200 g (7 oz) of sliced mozzarella cheese instead of the goats' cheese for a different flavour.

**3** Cut the peppers in half lengthways and remove the seeds. Leave the stalks attached but trim away any white membrane. Place the peppers on a barbecue grill cut side down and cook for 8–10 minutes until well charred. Cut each goat's cheese into 4 slices. Turn the peppers over, place a slice of goats' cheese in the centre of each, sprinkle with the thyme and olive oil and leave to cook for a further 10 minutes or until the peppers have softened and the goats' cheese has melted.

**4** Serve sprinkled with the chopped black olives and cracked black pepper, accompanied by the chilli relish.

# Grilled Haloumi Wrapped in Radicchio

**Preparation time:** 10 minutes
**Cooking time:** 6–8 minutes

Serves 4

250 g (8 oz) haloumi cheese
1½ tablespoons chopped oregano
2 tablespoons extra virgin olive oil
1 garlic clove, crushed
2 tablespoons lemon juice
1 large head of radicchio
salt and pepper

**1** Cut the haloumi into 4 equal pieces or into lots of small cubes. Mix together the oregano, olive oil, garlic and lemon juice in a bowl, add the haloumi pieces and toss to coat.

**2** Remove the stalk and core from the radicchio and gently pull the leaves apart. Lay 3–4 leaves on a work surface and place a quarter of the haloumi mixture in the centre. Wrap the radicchio around the cheese, and then over wrap in a piece of double thickness foil. Repeat with the remaining radicchio and cheese mixture.

**3** Place the parcels on a barbecue grill over a fairly low heat and cook for 3–4 minutes on each side. Remove from the heat and serve immediately.

**barbie tip**
These parcels make a tasty starter served with crusty bread, or can be eaten as a main course with new potatoes.

# Nut Koftas with Minted Yogurt

**Preparation time:** 15 minutes
**Cooking time:** 10 minutes

Serves 4

5–6 tablespoons vegetable oil
1 onion, chopped
½ teaspoon crushed chilli flakes
2 garlic cloves, coarsely chopped
1 tablespoon medium curry paste
425 g (14 oz) can cannellini beans, rinsed and drained
175 g (6 oz, ¾ cup) ground almonds
75 g (3 oz, ¾ cup) chopped honey-roasted or
    salted almonds
1 egg
200 ml (7 fl oz, 1 cup) yogurt
2 tablespoons chopped mint
1 tablespoon lemon juice
salt and pepper
mint sprigs, to garnish
warm Naan Bread (see page 158), to serve

**1** Heat 3 tablespoons of the oil in a frying pan, add the onion and fry for 4 minutes. Add the chilli flakes, garlic and curry paste and fry for a further 1 minute.

**2** Transfer to a food processor or blender with the beans, ground almonds, chopped almonds, egg and a little salt and pepper and process until the mixture starts to bind together.

**3** Using lightly floured hands, take about one-eighth of the mixture and mould around a skewer, forming it into a sausage about 2.5 cm (1 inch) thick. Make 7 more koftas in the same way. Place on a grill rack over moderate coals and brush with another tablespoon of the oil. Cook for about 5 minutes, until golden, turning once.

**4** Meanwhile, mix together the yogurt and mint in a small serving bowl and season to taste with salt and pepper. In a separate bowl, mix together the remaining oil, lemon juice and a little salt and pepper.

**5** Brush the koftas with the lemon dressing and serve with the yogurt dressing, on warm naan bread garnished with mint sprigs.

**barbie tip**
Be sure to oil the barbecue rack well before you put the koftas on it. They are a little crumbly and may be difficult to turn if they stick.

# Feta and Cherry Tomato Kebabs

**Preparation time:** 15 minutes, plus marinating
**Cooking time:** 4–6 minutes

Serves 4

2 thick slices of Italian bread
8 cherry tomatoes
8 sundried tomatoes in oil, drained
200 g (7 oz) feta cheese, cubed
4 black olives, plus extra to serve

MARINADE:
1 garlic clove, crushed
4 tablespoons lemon juice
2 teaspoons Pesto Sauce
6 tablespoons olive oil
salt

**1** To make the marinade, mix the garlic, lemon juice and salt into the pesto sauce. Whisk in the olive oil.

**2** Cut the bread into chunks and toss briefly in the marinade, then remove. Add the cherry tomatoes, sundried tomatoes and feta and leave for 30 minutes.

**3** Thread the ingredients on to skewers, starting with a cube of bread and finishing with an olive. Grill over hot coals for 2–3 minutes each side, basting with the marinade until the bread is crisp and the cheese is just beginning to melt. Serve with extra olives.

## Pesto Sauce

**Preparation time:** 10 minutes

Makes about 250 ml ($\frac{1}{4}$ pint, $\frac{2}{3}$ cup)

1 garlic clove, crushed
75 g (3 oz, $\frac{3}{4}$ cup) pine nuts
25 g (1 oz, 1 cup) basil leaves
150 ml ($\frac{1}{4}$ pint, $\frac{2}{3}$ cup) extra virgin olive oil
2 tablespoons freshly grated Parmesan cheese
salt and pepper

**1** Place the garlic, pine nuts and basil in a blender or food processor and process until fairly smooth (or grind using a pestle and mortar). Gradually beat in the oil, then stir in the cheese and adjust the seasoning to taste.

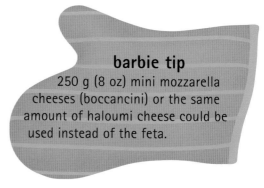

### barbie tip
250 g (8 oz) mini mozzarella cheeses (boccancini) or the same amount of haloumi cheese could be used instead of the feta.

# Mixed Vegetables with Green Olive and Walnut Paste

**Preparation time:** 1 hour
**Cooking time:** 10 minutes

Serves 4

1 large aubergine
2 red peppers
2 yellow peppers
2 courgettes
8 baby leeks
6 tablespoons olive oil
4 large slices of crusty bread

OLIVE AND WALNUT PASTE:
75 g (3 oz, ¾ cup) pitted green olives
75 g (3 oz, ¾ cup) walnut pieces
25 g (1 oz, ¼ cup) bottled pickled walnuts, drained
2 garlic cloves, crushed
25 g (1 oz, 1 cup) parsley
125 ml (4 fl oz, ½ cup) extra virgin olive oil
salt and pepper

**1** To make the olive and walnut paste, place the olives, fresh and pickled walnuts, garlic and parsley in a blender or food processor and process until finely chopped. Gradually add the olive oil through the feeder tube until the mixture forms a stiff paste. Scrape into a bowl and season with salt and pepper.

**2** Cut the aubergine into slices 1 cm (½ inch) thick. Cut the peppers in half, remove the seeds but leave the stalks on. Slice the courgettes lengthways into 5 mm (¼ inch) slices. Rinse the leeks well to remove any grit.

**3** Brush the aubergines, peppers, courgettes and leeks with the olive oil. Place on an oiled grill rack over moderately hot coals. Cook the aubergine and peppers for 6–8 minutes, the courgettes and leeks for 3 minutes, turning frequently, until tender. Brush the bread with any remaining olive oil and grill until golden. Spread the toast with the olive and walnut paste and top with the vegetables.

**barbie tip**
Choose a selection of vegetables in season to serve with this rich green olive and walnut paste. Asparagus and fennel are also excellent when barbecued.

# Asparagus with Balsamic Tomato Dressing

*Asparagus is perfect for the barbecue as it cooks quickly and easily. Serve this as an accompaniment, or as a starter with lots of warm bread to mop up the juices while you prepare the main course.*

**Preparation time:** 15 minutes
**Cooking time:** 5–6 minutes

Serves 4

2 tablespoons balsamic vinegar
1–2 garlic cloves, crushed
375 g (12 oz) tomatoes, skinned, deseeded and
    chopped
7 tablespoons olive oil
500 g (1 lb) young asparagus spears
50 g (2 oz, ½ cup) pine nuts, toasted
25 g (1 oz) Parmesan cheese, shaved into thin slivers
sea salt flakes and pepper

**1** Place the vinegar, garlic, chopped tomatoes and 5 tablespoons of the olive oil in a small bowl. Mix well to combine and set aside.

**2** Trim the asparagus spears to remove any tough fibrous stems. Brush them with the remaining olive oil and cook on an oiled barbecue grill over moderately hot coals for about 5–6 minutes, until tender.

**3** Divide the grilled asparagus between 4 warmed serving plates. Spoon over the balsamic vinegar and tomato dressing, top with the pine nuts and Parmesan slivers and sprinkle with the sea salt flakes and pepper. Serve at once.

**barbie tip**
Plainly grilled, asparagus is also delicious served with fish, poultry or meat.

# Sweetcorn with Skorthalia

**barbie tip**

Skorthalia is a garlic sauce which can also be served with other vegetables, or grilled meat or fish. It goes particularly well with barbecued courgette and fennel wedges.

**Preparation time:** 15 minutes
**Cooking time:** 30–40 minutes

Serves 4

4 whole corn cobs, with husks

SKORTHALIA:
50 g (2 oz, ½ cup) fresh white breadcrumbs
75 g (3 oz, ¼ cup plus 2 tablespoons) ground almonds
4 garlic cloves, crushed
2 tablespoons lemon juice
150 ml (¼ pint, ⅔ cup) extra virgin olive oil
salt and pepper

**1** To make the skorthalia, place the breadcrumbs in a bowl and cover with water. Soak for 5 minutes, then squeeze out the excess liquid and place the crumbs in a blender or food processor. Add the ground almonds, garlic and 1 tablespoon of the lemon juice. Process until mixed. With the motor running, gradually add the olive oil in a thin steady stream until the mixture resembles mayonnaise. Add more lemon juice and salt and pepper to taste.

**2** Pull down the outer leaves of the sweetcorn cobs and remove the inner skins. Pull the leaves back over the corn cobs. Place on a barbecue grill over hot coals. Cook for about 30–40 minutes, until the kernels are juicy and easily come away from the core.

**3** To serve, pull back the leaves of the corn cobs and spread with the skorthalia.

# Beetroot with Mustard and Walnut Sauce

**Preparation time:** 15 minutes
**Cooking time:** 40–50 minutes

Serves 4

75 g (3 oz, ¾ cup) walnut halves
175 g (6 oz, ¾ cup) crème fraîche
1½ tablespoons wholegrain mustard
3 tablespoons snipped chives, plus extra for garnish
8 raw beetroot
salt and pepper

**1** Roast the walnuts on a baking sheet in a preheated oven at 180°C (350°F), Gas Mark 4, for about 8–10 minutes until they are golden. Leave to cool, then chop roughly. Reserve 3 tablespoons of the nuts for garnish, and put the rest in a bowl.

**2** Stir in the crème fraîche, mustard and snipped chives. Season with salt and pepper to taste.

**3** Wrap each beetroot in a double thickness of foil. Place in the embers of the hot barbecue and cook for about 40–50 minutes, or until tender.

**4** Unwrap the foil, split open the beetroot and top with the sauce, the reserved walnuts and extra chives.

### barbie tip
This recipe is very economical of barbecue space as the beetroot are cooked in the coals, leaving the grill rack empty for other food.

# Radicchio with Pears and Roquefort

*The slight bitterness of the radicchio combines well with citrus-sweet baked pears and creamy sharp cheese to make a dish which is equally suitable as an unusual starter or as an ending to a rich meal.*

**Preparation time:** 5 minutes
**Cooking time:** 15–20 minutes

Serves 4
4 ripe pears, such as Conference
finely grated rind and juice of 2 oranges
4 tablespoons clear honey
4 small radicchio heads
1 tablespoon walnut oil
125 g (4 oz) Roquefort cheese, crumbled
pepper

**1** Cut each pear into quarters lengthways and remove the cores. Place the pears in a single layer on a large sheet of double thickness foil, turning up the edges slightly. Mix the orange rind and juice and honey in a jug and pour over the pears.

**2** Bring up the edges of the foil and press together to seal. Place the parcel on a barbecue grill over moderately hot coals and cook for about 15–20 minutes or until the pears are tender.

**3** About 6 minutes before the pears are ready, cook the radicchio. Cut each head into quarters, brush with the walnut oil and cook on the grill for 2–3 minutes on each side.

**4** To serve, divide the pears and their cooking juices between 4 plates. Add 4 radicchio quarters to each portion then sprinkle with the crumbled Roquefort and a little pepper.

**barbie tip**
Sadly the ruby-red colour of the radicchio is somewhat lost in cooking but the flavour is delicious none the less.

# Chinese Leaves Steamed with Shiitake Mushrooms

**Preparation time:** 10 minutes
**Cooking time:** 5–10 minutes

Serves 4

375 g (12 oz) Chinese leaves
125 g (4 oz) shiitake mushrooms, finely sliced
1 cm (½ inch) piece of fresh root ginger, peeled and
    finely shredded
1 garlic clove, crushed
½ tablespoon light soy sauce
2 teaspoons soft light brown sugar
1 green chilli, deseeded and finely chopped
1 teaspoon sesame oil
3 spring onions, finely chopped

**1** Shred the Chinese leaves into 1 cm
(½ inch) strips and place in a large bowl. Mix
all the other ingredients in a separate bowl.
Add to the Chinese leaves and toss lightly.

**2** Place a large piece of double thickness foil
on a work surface, then pile the mixture into
the centre. Bring up the edges and press to
seal. Cook the foil parcel on a barbecue grill
over hot coals for 5–10 minutes, shaking
occasionally, until the Chinese leaves and
mushrooms are tender.

**barbie tip**
Other varieties of mushrooms,
such as brown chestnuts or tender
oyster mushrooms, may be used
instead of shiitake.

# Barbecuing fruit and vegetables

Although when most people think of a barbecue they think of steaks and sausages, vegetables and fruits can make a valuable contribution to a barbecued meal. Succulent chargrilled vegetables will appeal to everyone. Think of melt-in-the-mouth aubergine slices, sweet baby peppers stuffed with goats' cheese and herbs, butter or golden sweetcorn cobs straight from the grill.

Many fruits are also great cooked over coals since barbecuing concentrates the flavours and lightly caramelizes the natural sugars.

## Vegetables for Barbecuing

**Asparagus** – Cook over medium coals until lightly charred and tender.

**Aubergines** – Choose from thick aubergine slices or wedges, or baby aubergines which can be cooked whole. Baste with oil during cooking.

**Beetroot** – Beetroot wedges or whole baby beetroot can be wrapped in foil and cooked on the grill rack or among the coals until soft.

**Courgettes** – Cut into chunks or thick slices, or cook baby courgettes whole. Great for kebabs or for marinating.

**Fennel** – Either cut the bulbs into wedges, keeping the root end intact, or separate into thick fleshy leaves. Cook over medium coals until tender, basting with oil or a marinade from time to time.

**Garlic** – Barbecued garlic is sweet and succulent, and loses all of its harsh flavour. Wrap the whole bulbs in foil

## Cooking Equipment

Some fruits and vegetables are too small or delicate to be cooked straight on the grill rack, but this doesn't mean they can't be barbecued.
**Skewers** are the obvious answer – simply thread small ingredients on wooden or metal skewers. They will not fall through the bars and they can be turned in batches, making cooking much easier.
**Perforated metal baskets** are also available for cooking vegetables on a barbecue. They sit on the grill rack and the small pieces of vegetable can be placed inside to cook. The baskets are usually large enough to accommodate quite a few vegetables at a time and the open top means they can be turned and stirred frequently.
**Flat wire baskets** are also suitable for vegetables. These come in two halves which are clipped together, sandwiching the food inside and making turning very easy.
**Foil parcels** are a useful aid to cooking fruits and vegetables. The sealed parcels are cooked on the grill rack over the coals and the food steams inside.

and cook on the grill rack or among the coals until soft and tender.

**Mushrooms** – Cook large field mushrooms whole, basting with oil or melted butter, or thread button mushrooms on to skewers. Great on mixed kebabs, or basted with garlic and herbs. Cook over medium coals.

**Onions** – Cut large onions into wedges, keeping the root end intact, or into squares for kebabs. Whole baby onions are also great on the barbie, but make sure they are cooked long enough to soften right through.

**Peppers** – Peppers are perfect for barbecuing. Cut them into squares for kebabs, or cook deseeded halves or quarters directly on the grill until softened.

**Potatoes** – Cut large potatoes into wedges or slices, or cook small potatoes whole on skewers. Potato skins are also very successful.

**Pumpkin** – Pumpkin becomes sweet when cooked on a barbecue and the flavours intensify. Cut into wedges, brush with oil and cook over medium coals.

**Squash** – Whole baby squash are great for kebabs, but larger squash, such as acorn or butternut should be cut into wedges and barbecued directly on the grill rack.

**Sweet potatoes** – Any of the potato recipes can be made with sweet potatoes instead.

## Hints and Tips

✳ Use barbecued fruit wedges, such as figs, apples and pears, to accompany meats.
✳ Clean off the barbie grill before cooking fruits for dessert.
✳ Thread small items on skewers to make turning easier and stop them dropping through the grill.
✳ Perforated metal baskets are great for all kinds of small ingredients.
✳ Most fruits and vegetables are best cooked over medium coals to give them time to become tender before they are too charred.
✳ Remember marinades are just as good with vegetables as meats and fish.
✳ Pep up a platter of barbecued vegetables with a flavoured oil or sauce. See chapter 10 for ideas.

**Sweetcorn** – Cook the cobs whole, or cut into chunks. The cobs can be barbecued naked and basted with oil or melted butter, or they can be cooked with their outer leaves intact to keep the kernels moist.

**Tomatoes** – Large beefsteak tomatoes can be cut in half and barbecued on the grill rack, or try cherry tomatoes on kebabs or simply cooked on skewers. Cook over medium coals just until the skins colour a little.

# Fruits for Barbecuing

**Apples** – Cut into rings or wedges, brush with oil or melted butter and cook until golden.

**Bananas** – Put whole bananas, skins and all, on to the grill rack and turn them occasionally until the skins are blackened all over. The fruit inside will be soft and sticky, perfect for topping with ice cream or cream.

**Figs** – Barbecued figs are sweet and soft. Good with both sweet and savoury dishes, they can be slit open and cooked on the grill rack, or wrapped in foil and steamed over hot coals.

**Mango** – The natural sugars in the fruit caramelize to give a lovely charred flavour.

**Nectarines and peaches** – Cut in half, remove the stones and cook until soft over medium coals.

**Pears** – Great for sweet and savoury dishes. Cut into quarters, remove the cores, brush with oil or melted butter and cook over medium coals. Alternatively, wrap in foil parcels and steam the pears on the barbecue.

**Pineapple** – Pineapple rings are robust enough to be cooked on the grill rack, where they will become charred and caramelized, or cook in foil parcels with flavourings.

**Strawberries** – Great for summer kebabs or foil parcels. Do not overcook or they will become slushy.

# chapter 8
# Salads and Accompaniments

A wonderful array of bread, pasta, potatoes, salads and vegetable side dishes to compliment barbecued food.

# Grissini

Preparation time: 20 minutes, plus proving
Cooking time: 5-8 minutes

Makes 16-20

15 g (½ oz, 1 tablespoon) fresh yeast, or 2 sachets easy-blend
    dried yeast
pinch of sugar
125 ml (4 fl oz, ½ cup) warm water
175 g (6 oz, 1½ cups) Italian flour
1 tablespoon olive oil
1 teaspoon coarse sea salt
slices of prosciutto, cut into strips, to serve

FLAVOURINGS:
coarse sea salt
sesame seeds
poppy seeds
cracked black pepper

1 If you are using fresh yeast, cream it with the sugar
in a medium bowl then whisk in the warm water. Leave
for 10 minutes until frothy. For easy-blend yeast, follow
packet instructions.

2 Sift the flour into a large bowl and make a well in the
centre. Pour in the yeast mixture, olive oil and salt. Mix
together with a round-bladed knife, then with your hand,
until the dough comes together.

3 Tip the dough out on to a floured surface. Wash
and dry your hands, then knead the dough for about
10 minutes until it is smooth and elastic. Place it in a
clean, oiled bowl, cover with a damp tea towel and leave
to rise until doubled in size. This will take about an hour.

4 Working on a well-floured surface, roll the dough out
thinly to a rectangle. Cut it into 5 mm (¼ inch) strips,
following the long side of the rectangle. Lightly roll
these strips and taper the ends.

5 Brush the grissini lightly with water and sprinkle with
the flavouring of your choice. Put them on a baking
sheet and bake in a preheated oven, 200°C (400°F), Gas
mark 6, for 5-8 minutes until crisp and brown. Leave to
cool completely.

6 To serve, twist strips of prosciutto around the grissini.

**barbie tip**
Nothing like the ones in
packets, these grissini are fun to
make and great served with drinks
as the barbie heats up.

# Olives Marinated with Asian Flavours

**Preparation time:** 5 minutes

Serves 8

250 g (8 oz, 2 cups) mixed green and black olives
1 garlic clove, crushed
1 teaspoon grated ginger
2 kaffir lime leaves, shredded
2 red chillies, bruised
2 tablespoons dark soy sauce
4 tablespoons extra virgin olive oil

**barbie tip**
If you can't get lime leaves, use the grated rind of 1 lime instead.

**1** Place the olives in a bowl, add the remaining ingredients and stir well. Cover and refrigerate for up to 1 week.

# Bruschetta with Grilled Pepper and Hazelnuts

**Preparation time:** 10 minutes
**Cooking time:** 15 minutes

Serves 4

4 thick slices of day-old rustic bread
2 garlic cloves, halved
extra virgin olive oil, to drizzle

TOPPING:
1 yellow pepper, cored, deseeded and quartered
1 red pepper, cored, deseeded and quartered
2 tablespoons hazelnut oil
2 garlic cloves, sliced
1 tablespoon grated lemon rind
25 g (1 oz, ¼ cup) sultanas
25 g (1 oz, ¼ cup) flaked hazelnuts
175 g (6 oz) salad leaves (such as baby spinach, rocket, frisée)

**1** To make the topping, grill the pepper quarters, skin-side up, for 6–8 minutes until charred and tender. Put into a plastic bag and set aside until cool enough to handle. Peel off the skin and slice the flesh.

**2** Heat the oil in a frying pan, add the garlic, lemon rind, sultanas and hazelnuts and fry gently for 5 minutes until golden. Add the salad leaves and cook over a low heat for 3 minutes, or until just wilted.

**3** Meanwhile, prepare the bruschetta. Toast the bread lightly on both sides. Immediately rub the toast all over with the garlic cloves and drizzle with olive oil.

**4** Divide the salad mixture between the bruschetta and top with the grilled peppers. Serve at once.

**barbie tip**
If the barbie is ready in time, you could cook the peppers and/or toast the bread on it.

# Naan Bread

**Preparation time:** 20 minutes, plus proving
**Cooking time:** 25 minutes

Makes 4

1 teaspoon dried yeast
1 teaspoon sugar
50 ml (2 fl oz, ¼ cup) warm milk
250 g (8 oz, 2 cups) plain flour
½ teaspoon salt
1 tablespoon vegetable oil
1 egg, beaten
4 tablespoons natural yogurt

**1** Sprinkle the yeast and sugar over the milk. Mix, cover and keep warm for 15–20 minutes, until frothy.

**2** Sift the flour and salt into a large bowl, make a well in the centre and add the rest of the ingredients, plus the yeast mixture. Mix, gradually incorporating the flour until the dough forms a soft ball. Turn out on to a floured work surface, knead for 10 minutes until smooth, then place in an oiled bowl. Cover and leave to rise in a warm place for 1 hour or until the dough has doubled in bulk.

**3** Return to the floured surface, punch down to remove the air, then knead for 5 minutes more. Divide into 4, roll into 20 x 12 cm (8 x 5 inch) tear shapes, place on an oiled baking sheet, cover and leave to rise for 25 minutes in a warm place.

**4** Heat a cast iron pan and cook each piece of dough for 3 minutes. Then place them under a grill for 2–3 minutes, until golden and spotty on top.

**barbie tip**
The naan dough can be flavoured with a handful of fennel or cumin seeds before cooking.

# Olive, Caper and Sundried Tomato Focaccia

**Preparation time:** 25 minutes, plus proving
**Cooking time:** 20–25 minutes

**Makes 2 thin 25 cm (10 inch) loaves**

25 g (1 oz) fresh yeast or 1 sachet easy-blend dried
   yeast
pinch of sugar
450 ml (¾ pint, 1¾ cups) warm water
750 g (1½ lb, 6 cups) plain white flour, plus extra
   for dusting
125 ml (4 fl oz, ½ cup) good olive oil
50 g (2 oz, ½ cup) sundried tomatoes (the dried kind),
   soaked and sliced
2 tablespoons salted capers, rinsed
250 g (8 oz, 2 cups) black or green olives, pitted
coarse sea salt

**1** If you are using fresh yeast, cream it together with the sugar in a medium bowl then whisk in the warm water. Leave for 10 minutes until frothy. For dried yeast, refer to the packet instructions.

**2** Sift the flour into a large bowl and make a well in the centre. Pour in the yeast mixture and 3 tablespoons of the olive oil. Mix with a round-bladed knife, then your hands, until the dough comes together.

**3** Tip out the dough on to a floured surface. Wash and dry your hands and knead the dough for 10 minutes until it is smooth and elastic. Place the dough in a clean, oiled bowl, cover with a damp tea towel and leave to rise in a warm place until doubled in size – about 1½ hours.

**4** Lightly oil two shallow 25 cm (10 inch) pie or pizza plates. Knock down the dough and knead in the sundried tomatoes, capers and half of the olives. Divide the dough in half. Working on a floured surface, shape each piece into a round and roll out to a 25 cm (10 inch) circle. Place them on the pie or pizza plates. Cover with a damp tea towel and leave to rise for 30 minutes.

**5** Remove the tea towel and make dimples all over the surface of the dough with your fingertips. They can be quite deep. Cover the dough again and leave to rise until doubled in size – about 2 hours.

**6** Pour over the remaining oil, scatter with the remaining olives and sprinkle generously with salt. Spray the focaccia with water and bake in a preheated oven at 200°C (400°F), Gas Mark 6, for 20–25 minutes. Transfer to a wire rack to cool.

**barbie tip**
Eat the focaccia the same day or freeze as soon as they have cooled.

# Spiced Coleslaw

**Preparation time:** 15 minutes

Serves 4

¼–½ white cabbage or cabbage heart
1 unpeeled dessert apple, cored and diced
2 carrots, grated
2 tablespoons diced gherkins
2 teaspoons capers
2 tablespoons chopped parsley

SPICED DRESSING:
3 tablespoons Mayonnaise (see page 187)
½ teaspoon curry powder
½ teaspoon ground nutmeg
½ teaspoon paprika
1 teaspoon English mustard
1 tablespoon olive oil
1 tablespoon lemon juice
salt and pepper

**1** Make the dressing first by whisking all the ingredients together.

**2** Shred the cabbage finely by hand or with a food processor. Add the apple and carrots to the dressing, together with the gherkins, capers and parsley. Mix together thoroughly, then add the cabbage and mix again.

**barbie tip**
Avoid making the coleslaw too far ahead, as the cabbage and other ingredients should remain as fresh and crisp as possible.

# Orange and Olive Salad

*The oranges that work best for this salad have a sharp flavour, not a sweet taste. The olives should be large and fleshy.*

**Preparation time:** 10–15 minutes
**Cooking time:** 5 minutes

**Serves 4**

2 teaspoons cumin seeds
4 large oranges
125 g (4 oz, 1 cup) green olives, pitted and halved
50 ml (2 fl oz, ¼ cup) olive oil
1 tablespoon harissa (optional)
1 crisp lettuce, torn into bite-sized pieces
salt
dill sprigs, to garnish

**1** Heat a small heavy-based frying pan, add the cumin seeds and dry-fry until fragrant. Tip into a grinder and grind to a powder.

**2** Remove the rind from 1 of the oranges with a zester and set aside. Peel the oranges with a sharp knife, carefully removing all the pith. Working over a bowl to catch the juice, cut out the segments from the oranges and discard any pips. Put the oranges and olives into a bowl with the juice.

**3** Whisk or shake together the oil, harissa, if using, and roasted cumin. Add salt to taste, then pour the dressing over the oranges and olives and toss together.

**4** Arrange the lettuce leaves in a serving dish. Add the orange and olive mixture. Garnish with the reserved orange rind and sprigs of dill and serve.

### barbie tip
Harissa is a fiery sauce made of red peppers, red chillies, garlic and spices. It gives this salad an extra kick. However, if unavailable, substitute a few drops of Tabasco sauce.

# Cucumber, Radish and Dill Salad

**Preparation time:** 15 minutes, plus salting

Serves 4–6

2 cucumbers
6 tablespoons sea salt
1 bunch of radishes, trimmed and thinly sliced
1 egg yolk
1 tablespoon coarse grain mustard
1 tablespoon clear honey
2 tablespoons lemon juice
3 tablespoons olive oil
3 tablespoons chopped dill
pepper

**barbie tip**
Omit the honey and replace the dill with 3 tablespoons of parsley, tarragon or basil for a different flavour.

**1** Cut both the cucumbers in half lengthways, scoop out the seeds and slice very thinly.

**2** Layer the cucumber slices in a colander and sprinkle with the salt. Set the colander over a plate or in the sink to catch the juices and leave for 1–1½ hours. Rinse well under cold water, drain and pat the slices dry with a clean tea towel. Place in a salad bowl and add the radishes.

**3** Place the egg yolk in a small bowl with the mustard, honey, pepper and lemon juice. Whisk well to combine. Continue to whisk while gradually adding the oil in a thin stream until well amalgamated. Then, stir in the chopped dill. and add to the cucumber and radishes, toss well and serve.

# Watercress and Pomegranate Salad

*This is a colourful and unusual salad, perfumed with fragrant rosewater and strewn with pomegranate seeds and orange segments. It is a stunning accompaniment to barbecued meat and game.*

**Preparation time:** 15 minutes

Serves 4

1 pomegranate
1 bunch of watercress, broken into sprigs
4 oranges
1 teaspoon rosewater
5 tablespoons olive oil
1 tablespoon raspberry vinegar
$\frac{1}{2}$ teaspoon pink peppercorns in brine, drained
sea salt flakes

**1** Break open the pomegranate and remove the seeds, discarding the bitter yellow pith. Place the seeds in a large bowl with the watercress.

**2** Finely grate the rind from 2 of the oranges and set aside. Segment all the oranges and carefully remove the membrane around each segment, catching any juices in the bowl containing the pomegranate and watercress. Place the orange segments in the bowl with the watercress.

**3** In a separate bowl, combine the rosewater, olive oil, raspberry vinegar, pink peppercorns and reserved grated orange rind. Mix well, pour over the salad, season with a few sea salt flakes and serve.

**barbie tip**
If you can't get rosewater, orange flower water can be used instead. Replace the raspberry vinegar for white wine vinegar.

# Tomato and Green Bean Salad

Preparation time: 10 minutes
Cooking time: 2 minutes

Serves 4

250 g (8 oz) mixed red and yellow baby tomatoes
    (plum tomatoes, if possible)
250 g (8 oz) thin green beans, trimmed
handful of mint, chopped
1 garlic clove, crushed
4 tablespoons extra virgin olive oil
1 tablespoon balsamic vinegar
salt and pepper

**1** Cut the baby tomatoes in half and place in a large bowl.

**2** Blanch the green beans in a saucepan of lightly salted boiling water for 2 minutes, then drain well and place in the bowl with the tomatoes.

**3** Add the chopped mint, garlic, olive oil and balsamic vinegar. Season with salt and pepper and mix well. Serve warm or cold.

### barbie tip
This dish is also delicious if you roast the tomatoes lightly before adding to the salad. Leave them whole and thread on to skewers. Cook for 1–2 minutes on each side over moderately hot coals.

# Green Salad with a Mixed Herb Sauce

**Preparation time:** 10 minutes

Serves 4

1 round lettuce
1 batavia lettuce
125 g (4 oz, 1 cup) corn salad

HERB SAUCE:
2 eggs, hard boiled
2 tablespoons double cream
2 tablespoons olive oil
2 teaspoons white wine vinegar
1 tablespoon chopped chives
1 tablespoon chopped dill
1 tablespoon chopped tarragon
salt and pepper

**1** Break the round lettuce leaves in pieces and pile in a salad bowl. Using only the pale green inner leaves of the batavia lettuce, scatter them over the lettuce and put the corn salad on top.

**2** To make the herb sauce, separate the whites and yolks of the hard boiled eggs. Chop the egg whites and scatter over the green salad. Mash the egg yolks to a paste with the cream, and stir in the oil very gradually.

**3** Add the vinegar slowly and stir until blended. Add salt and pepper to taste, and stir in the herbs. Pour the herb sauce over the salad and mix well.

**barbie tip**
Batavia, also called scarole, is a type of endive. Though it is slightly less curly than endive, it has a similar, slightly bitter taste which provides an interesting contrast of flavour in green salads.

# Greek Country Salad

*This traditional salad immediately evokes the atmosphere of Greece. It is served in Greek tavernas all over the world.*

**Preparation time:** 25–30 minutes, plus standing and salting

**Serves 4**

4 tablespoons olive oil
1 tablespoon red wine vinegar
1 garlic clove, crushed
½ cucumber, peeled if preferred
1 small round lettuce, torn
1 small Cos lettuce, shredded
3 firm but ripe tomatoes, cut into wedges
1 Spanish onion, thinly sliced into rings
1 green pepper, cored, deseeded and thinly sliced into rings
125 g (4 oz) feta cheese, crumbled
12 or more olives (Kalamata, if possible)
1–2 tablespoons coarsely chopped parsley
2 teaspoons chopped oregano
salt and pepper

**1** Whisk together the oil, vinegar, garlic and salt and pepper to taste. Cover and set aside for 1 hour.

**2** Halve the cucumber lengthways, scoop out the seeds and cut in thin slices. Sprinkle with salt and leave to drain for 30 minutes. Rinse the cucumber and dry with absorbent kitchen paper.

**3** Whisk the oil and vinegar again, then toss a little of it with the lettuce in a bowl. Layer the tomatoes, cucumber, onion, green pepper, cheese and olives on the lettuce.

**4** Pour over the remaining dressing, then scatter over the chopped parsley and oregano and serve.

### barbie tip
Serve with simple lamb, chicken or prawn kebabs, threaded with onion and pepper squares, and toasted pitta breads.

# Orecchiette, Broad Bean and Pecorino Salad

*'Orecchiette', meaning 'little ears', are pasta shapes with a soft creamy texture and go very well with this mixture of sharp Pecorino cheese and sweet baby broad beans.*

**Preparation time:** 10 minutes
**Cooking time:** 15 minutes

Serves 4

750 g (1½ lb) fresh young broad beans in the pod or
    250 g (8 oz) frozen broad beans, thawed
5 tablespoons extra virgin olive oil
500 g (1 lb) orecchiette or similar short pasta shapes
75 g (3 oz) Pecorino cheese, grated
50 g (2 oz, ½ cup) pitted black olives, finely chopped
5 tablespoons chopped flat leaf parsley
1 tablespoon balsamic vinegar
salt and pepper

**1** Shell the broad beans, if fresh. Bring a saucepan of lightly salted water to the boil, add the fresh or thawed frozen beans and blanch for 1 minute. Drain, refresh under cold water, then drain again. Pop the beans out of their shells.

**2** Bring a large saucepan of boiling water to the boil with a little oil and salt, drop in the pasta and cook for 12–15 minutes, or until just tender. Drain the pasta in a colander, refresh under cold water and drain thoroughly.

**3** Tip the pasta into a large salad bowl and add the remaining ingredients. Toss well, add plenty of pepper and serve.

**barbie tip**
This substantial salad makes a nice accompaniment to a selection of barbecued vegetables.

# Tabbouleh and Fennel Salad

*Fennel adds crunch to this moist bulgar wheat salad.*

**Preparation time:** 15 minutes, plus soaking and standing

Serves 6

250 g (8 oz, 2 cups) bulgar wheat
1 fennel bulb, very finely sliced
1 red onion, finely sliced
5 tablespoons chopped mint
5 tablespoons chopped parsley
2 tablespoons fennel seeds, crushed
2 tablespoons olive oil
finely grated rind and juice of 2 lemons
salt and pepper

**1** Place the bulgar wheat in a bowl, add enough cold water to cover, then set aside for 30 minutes, until all the water has been absorbed. Line a colander with muslin or a clean tea towel. Drain the bulgar wheat into the colander, then gather up the sides of the cloth or tea towel and squeeze to extract as much of the liquid as possible from the bulgar wheat. Tip the wheat into a salad bowl.

**2** Stir in the fennel, onion, mint, parsley, fennel seeds, oil, lemon rind and half the lemon juice. Season with salt and pepper to taste. Cover and set aside for 30 minutes to allow the flavours to develop, then taste the salad and add more lemon juice if required.

**barbie tip**
To make a couscous and celery salad, substitute 250 g (8 oz, 2 cups) of quick-cooking couscous for the bulgar wheat and 6 celery sticks, finely sliced, for the fennel. Proceed as in the main recipe.

# Grilled Sweet Potato and Aioli

**Preparation time:** 15 minutes
**Cooking time:** 10 minutes

Serves 4

500 g (1 lb) sweet potatoes, scrubbed
4 tablespoons olive oil

AIOLI:
4–6 garlic cloves, crushed
2 egg yolks
2 tablespoons lemon juice, plus extra to taste
300 ml (½ pint, 1½ cups) extra virgin olive oil
salt and pepper

**1** To make the aioli, place the garlic and egg yolks in a blender or food processor, add the lemon juice and process briefly to mix. With the motor running, gradually add the olive oil in a thin steady stream until the mixture forms a thick cream. Add salt and pepper to taste and stir in more lemon juice if you like. Scrape the aioli into a bowl and set aside.

**2** To prepare the sweet potatoes, cut each potato into 5 mm (¼ inch) slices, brush with the olive oil and place on an oiled barbecue grill over moderately hot coals. Grill for about 5 minutes on each side until tender. Serve hot with the aioli.

**barbie tip**
Aioli, or garlic mayonnaise, is served here with delicious nutty sweet potatoes. You could also add 15 g (½ oz, 1 tablespoon) chopped mixed herbs to the aioli.

# Flageolet Bean and Roasted Vegetable Salad

**Preparation time:** 15 minutes
**Cooking time:** 40 minutes

Serves 4

1 aubergine
1 red pepper, halved, cored and deseeded
1 yellow pepper, halved, cored and deseeded
1 courgette
4 garlic cloves
4 tablespoons extra virgin olive oil
1 teaspoon coarse sea salt
300 g (10 oz, 1¼ cups) cooked flageolet beans
2 tablespoons chopped mixed herbs (such as parsley
    and oregano or coriander and mint)
6 tablespoons Classic Vinaigrette (see page 188)
pepper
mint leaves, to garnish

**1** Cut all the vegetables into strips and place in a roasting tin. Add the garlic cloves. Sprinkle over the olive oil, sea salt and pepper.

**2** Place in a preheated oven at 200°C (400°F), Gas Mark 6, and roast for 40 minutes. Transfer to a shallow bowl and leave to cool.

**3** Add the beans and toss lightly. Stir the herbs into the vinaigrette, pour over the salad and serve garnished with mint.

**barbie tip**
Other vegetables also work well in this salad, including fennel, tomatoes, baby squash and mild chillies.

# chapter 9
# Delicious Desserts

End your barbecue on a high with one of these glamorous, yet surprisingly simple desserts.

# Bananas with Mascarpone and Rum Cream

Preparation time: 5 minutes
Cooking time: 10–12 minutes

Serves 4

1–2 tablespoons caster sugar
$\frac{1}{2}$ teaspoon ground cinnamon
2 teaspoons rum
250 g (8 oz) mascarpone cheese
8 small bananas

**1** Mix the sugar, cinnamon and rum in a bowl. Stir in the mascarpone, mix well and set aside.

**2** Place the whole, unpeeled bananas on a barbecue grill over hot coals and cook for 10–12 minutes, turning the bananas as the skins darken, until they are black all over and the flesh is very tender.

**3** To serve, split the bananas open and spread the flesh with the mascarpone cream.

**barbie tip**
If you don't have any mascarpone, simply serve the barbecued bananas with cream.

# Barbecued Fruits with Palm Sugar

**Preparation time:** 10 minutes, plus cooling
**Cooking time:** 6–8 minutes

Serves 4

25 g (1 oz, 2 tablespoons) palm sugar
grated rind and juice of 1 lime
2 tablespoons water
1/2 teaspoon cracked black peppercorns
500 g (1 lb) mixed prepared fruits (such as pineapple
  slices, mango wedges and peaches)

TO SERVE:
cinnamon or vanilla ice cream
lime slices

**1** Warm the sugar, lime rind and juice, water
and peppercorns together in a small pan until
the sugar has dissolved. Plunge the base of the
pan into iced water to cool.

**2** Brush the cooled syrup over the prepared
fruits and barbecue for 3–4 minutes on each
side until charred and tender. Serve with
scoops of cinnamon or vanilla ice cream and
slices of lime.

### barbie tip
If you are watching your weight,
serve the barbecued fruits with a
little low-fat natural yogurt.

# Grilled Fruit Skewers with Rum Butter Glaze

**Preparation time:** 25 minutes
**Cooking time:** 5–7 minutes

**Serves:** 4

1.1 kg (2 lb) assorted fruits in season (e.g. mango, papaya, peach, strawberries, oranges, apples or pears)
lime or lemon juice, for brushing

RUM BUTTER GLAZE:
75 g (3 oz, ¼ cup plus 2 tablespoons) butter
2 tablespoons muscovado sugar
1 tablespoon rum or other liqueur

**1** To make the rum butter glaze, melt the butter in a small saucepan together with the muscovado sugar. Stir in the rum (or liqueur of your choice).

**2** If using wooden skewers, soak them in cold water for 30 minutes. Prepare the fruit according to type and cut it into evenly sized pieces. Thread on to 8 skewers, alternating the different types of fruit, to create a colourful effect.

**3** Brush all the fruit with lime or lemon juice and then brush them with the flavoured butter glaze. Cook on a barbecue grill over moderately hot coals for 2–3 minutes on each side, brush with more butter and then cook the skewers for 1 minute more.

**4** Serve the hot grilled skewers at once, together with a separate bowl of cream, mascarpone, or yogurt for dipping if liked.

**barbie tip**
Choose varieties of fruit that will take roughly the same amount of time to cook and cut them into pieces of equal size.

# Grilled Honeyed Peaches

*Sweet, fragrant peaches served hot from the grill with a Marsala syrup and crunch amaretti biscuits make a very simple but spectacular dessert.*

**Preparation time:** 15 minutes
**Cooking time:** 5–7 minutes

Serves 4

4 ripe peaches
300 ml (½ pint, 1¼ cups) Marsala
4 tablespoons honey
1 strip of orange rind
25 g (1 oz, 2 tablespoons) butter, melted
4 amaretti biscuits
vanilla ice cream or crème fraîche, to serve

**1** Cut a small cross in the top and bottom of each peach and place it in a pan of boiling water, leave for 20 seconds and transfer with a slotted spoon to a bowl of cold water. Peel, cut in half lengthways and remove the stone.

**2** Place the Marsala, honey and orange rind in a small saucepan, bring to the boil, then simmer for 2 minutes. Add the peach halves and simmer for 3–4 minutes until just tender. Remove the pan from the heat and leave the peaches to cool in the syrup.

**barbie tip**
Use very ripe peaches as they have the best flavour, but take care when turning them as they will be soft.

**3** Remove the peaches with a slotted spoon and place the remaining syrup in a small pan. Bring to the boil and reduce by half.

**4** Brush the peaches with the melted butter and place on the preheated barbecue for 5–7 minutes, turning once.

**5** Transfer the hot peaches to serving plates, spoon over a little of the reduced syrup and crumble over the amaretti biscuits. Serve with vanilla ice cream or crème fraîche.

# Figs and Blackberries on Toast

*Hot, squidgy figs and blackberries baked in liqueur are served with crispy cinnamon brioche toast to mop up the delicious cooking juices. Great for dessert or a barbecue brunch.*

**Preparation time:** 5–10 minutes
**Cooking time:** 8–10 minutes

Serves 4

12 ripe figs
125 g (4 oz, 1 cup) blackberries
pared rind and juice of 2 oranges
2 tablespoons crème de cassis
1 tablespoon caster sugar
½ teaspoon cinnamon
25 g (1 oz, 2 tablespoons) butter, melted
4 slices brioche or white bread
fromage frais or Greek yogurt, to serve (optional)

**1** Cut the figs into quarters, slicing almost but not all the way through, so the quarters fall back like flower petals. Cut 4 squares of double thickness foil and place 3 figs and a quarter of the blackberries on each.

**2** Cut the orange rind into thin julienne strips. Place in a bowl, stir in the orange juice and crème de cassis and divide between the fig parcels. Bring up the edges of the foil and press to seal.

**3** Mix the sugar, cinnamon and melted butter in a bowl and brush over one side of each brioche or bread slice.

**4** Cook the fig parcels on a barbecue grill over moderately hot coals for about 8–10 minutes, or until the figs are hot and slightly soft. Towards the end of the cooking time, add the buttered brioche or bread slices to the grill and toast until golden.

**5** Serve the cinnamon toast on individual plates, topped with the figs and blackberries. Add a spoonful of fromage frais or Greek yogurt, if liked.

### barbie tip
Crème de cassis is a syrup made from blackcurrants. It is usually non-alcoholic, though there is an alcoholic version.

# Rum-flambéed Pineapple Parcels

**Preparation time:** 15 minutes
**Cooking time:** 10–15 minutes

Serves 4

1 ripe pineapple, peeled
50 g (2 oz, ¼ cup) butter
75 g (3 oz, ¼ cup plus 2 tablespoons) light muscovado sugar
4 tablespoons dark rum
50 g (2 oz, ½ cup) pecan nuts, toasted and coarsely chopped
crème fraîche, to serve

**1** Cut the pineapple into 8 even slices, then remove the cores with a small pastry cutter to make rings.

**2** Using a double thickness of foil, cut out 4 foil squares, each large enough to hold 2 pineapple rings in a loose parcel. Place 2 rings on each square.

**3** Melt the butter in a small pan, stir in the sugar and cook gently until the sugar has dissolved. Divide between the parcels, then bring the edges of the foil together and press to seal.

**4** Cook on a grill rack over moderately hot coals for 10–15 minutes.

**5** When the pineapple is cooked, open the packages carefully, spoon 1 tablespoon of rum into each and ignite with a match. Scatter over the chopped pecans and serve at once with crème fraîche.

**barbie tip**
Because the pineapple is cooked in individual portions, the rum can be omitted from children's parcels.

# Baked Blueberry Parcels with Almond Cream

**Preparation time:** 15 minutes, plus draining time
**Cooking time:** 10 minutes

**Serves:** 6–8

750 g (1½ lb, 6 cups) fresh blueberries
6–8 tablespoons vanilla sugar (see barbie tip)
6–8 tablespoons créme de cassis
single cream, to serve (optional)

ALMOND CREAM:
750 g (1½ lb, 3 cups) ground almonds
1 kg (2 lb) mascarpone
3 egg yolks
100 g (3½ oz, 1 cup) caster sugar
125 ml (4 fl oz, 1 cup) double cream
2 tablespoons Amaretto

**1** To make the almond cream, first line an 18 cm (7 inch) sieve with a piece of muslin large enough to overhang the edge by about 10 cm (4 inches). Place the lined sieve over a bowl.

**2** In a mixing bowl, beat the ground almonds with the mascarpone. In a separate bowl, beat the egg yolks with the sugar until pale and fluffy. Fold into the mascarpone mixture.

**3** Whip the cream in another bowl until it forms soft peaks. Fold into the mascarpone with the Amaretto. Turn the mixture into the lined sieve, fold the excess muslin over, cover with a small plate and set a small weight on top. Place in the refrigerator for 6–8 hours or overnight, to drain.

**4** The blueberries are cooked in individual foil purses. For each purse you will require a 33 x 33 cm (13 x 13 inch) square of double foil. Heap a quarter of the blueberries in the centre of each foil square and turn up the edges of the foil to form a lip. Sprinkle the blueberries with 1 tablespoon of the vanilla sugar. Drizzle 1 tablespoon of the créme de cassis over the top, bring up the edges of the foil to make a parcel and press together to seal.

**5** Cook the sealed foil parcels on a barbecue grill over moderately hot coals for 8–10 minutes.

**6** Unmould the almond cream on to a large plate. Serve portions of the cream beside the blueberries and a jug of single cream, if liked.

### barbie tip
To make vanilla sugar, just steep one or two vanilla pods in a jar of plain sugar – the sugar will be deliciously scented and you can top up the jar with more sugar as required.

# Fresh Blueberry Cheesecake

**Preparation time:** 20 minutes, plus chilling
**Cooking time:** 5 minutes

Serves 8

1 tablespoon sugar
1 tablespoon water
250 g (8 oz, 2 cups) blueberries

BISCUIT BASE:
125 g (4 oz, 1 cup) digestive biscuits, crushed
75 g (3 oz, ¼ cup plus 2 tablespoons) caster sugar
1 teaspoon ground allspice
75 g (3 oz, ¼ cup plus 2 tablespoons) butter
1½ tablespoons apricot jam

FILLING:
1 tablespoon powdered gelatine
125 ml (4 fl oz, ½ cup) orange juice
150 g (5 oz, ½ cup plus 2 tablespoons) light
   brown sugar
2 tablespoons grated orange rind
425 g (14 oz) cream cheese
425 g (14 oz) ricotta
125 ml (4 fl oz, ½ cup) double cream, whipped

**1** To make the biscuit base, mix the biscuit crumbs in a bowl with the caster sugar and allspice. Melt the butter and jam in a small saucepan, then stir into the crumb mixture. Press into the bottom and up the sides of a greased and lined 20 cm (8 inch) springform cake tin. Refrigerate.

**2** Place the sugar in a saucepan with the water and heat gently to dissolve the sugar. Add half of the blueberries and simmer gently for 2 minutes. Remove from the heat and leave to cool.

**3** To make the filling, dissolve the gelatine in the orange juice in a bowl set over a saucepan of simmering water. Stir in the brown sugar and orange rind. Add the cheeses and beat thoroughly. Reserve a little cream and fold the rest into the filling.

**4** Strain the cooked blueberries. Spread the over the biscuit base, cover with the cheese filling, and top with the remaining fresh blueberries and cream. Chill for 5–6 hours.

### barbie tip
To make Fresh Raspberry Cheesecake, replace the blueberries with a similar quantity of raspberries and simmer in the syrup for just 30 seconds. Continue as in the recipe.

# Chocolate and Praline Truffle Terrine

**Preparation time:** 20 minutes, plus chilling

**Serves 6–8**

375 g (12 oz) dark chocolate, broken into squares
2 tablespoons water
175 ml (6 fl oz, ¾ cup) double cream
75 g (3 oz, ¼ cup plus 2 tablespoons) unsalted butter
1–2 tablespoons rum
75 g (3 oz, ⅓ cup) good quality candied peel (optional)
fresh fruit, to serve

PRALINE:
125 g (4 oz, ½ cup) sugar
125 g (4 oz, 1 cup) whole blanched almonds

**1** Grease and line a 20 x 10 cm (8 x 4 inch) loaf tin with non-stick baking paper, and oil a baking sheet.

**2** To make the praline, combine the sugar and almonds in a small, heavy saucepan. Heat gently until the sugar melts, stirring frequently. Continue to cook, stirring occasionally, until the sugar turns a deep golden brown and registers 165°C (330°F) on a sugar thermometer. Immediately remove from the heat and pour the mixture on to the oiled baking sheet, spreading it out slightly. Leave to cool. When the praline is completely cold, crush it into small pieces.

**3** Melt the broken chocolate with the measured water in a heatproof bowl over a saucepan of barely simmering water. Remove from the heat and leave to cool slightly.

**4** Whip the cream in a bowl until it forms soft peaks. In a separate bowl, cream the butter until soft and fluffy, then slowly stir in the chocolate mixture, followed by the rum. Fold in the cream, crushed praline and the candied peel, if using. Pour the mixture into the lined loaf tin. Level the top, cover and place in the refrigerator for 2–3 hours.

**5** To serve, unmould the terrine on to a platter and cut into thin slices. Serve seasonal fresh fruits as an accompaniment.

**barbie tip**
Be sure to use good quality chocolate for this rich and dark dessert – it should have a minimum of 50 per cent cocoa solids.

# Coffee Meringues

**Preparation time:** 35–40 minutes
**Cooking time:** 1½ hours
**Serves:** 6

MERINGUES
2 egg whites
125 g (3½ oz, ½ cup) caster sugar
1 tablespoon instant coffee powder

COFFEE CREAM FILLING
250–300 ml (8–10 fl oz, 1–1¼ cups) double cream
2 tablespoons Tia Maria or other coffee-flavoured liqueur
pistachios or almonds, toasted, to decorate

**1** Line 2 baking sheets with nonstick paper or baking parchment.

**2** Draw six 7.5 cm (3 inch) circles and six 5 cm (2 inch) circles on the paper with a pencil.

**3** Whisk the egg whites until stiff, then whisk in the sugar 1 tablespoon at a time. Add the coffee powder and continue whisking until the meringue is very stiff and holds its shape.

**4** Spoon into a piping bag fitted with a 1 cm (½ inch) plain nozzle and pipe over the circles.

**5** Bake in a preheated over at 110°C (225°F) Gas Mark ½ for 1½ hours until crisp. Peel the paper carefully off the meringues, then cool on a rack.

**6** Whip the cream and liqueur together in a bowl until stiff. Spoon into a piping bag fitted with a large fluted nozzle and pipe three-quarters of the cream on to the larger meringue circles.

**7** Top with the small circles, then pipe a whirl on each one with the remaining cream to serve. Decorate with toasted pistachios or almonds.

**barbie tip**
To freeze, open-freeze until solid, then pack carefully in a rigid container, separating each one with an interleaving sheet of kitchen foil. Seal, label and return to the freezer for up to 3 months.

# Tiramisu with Raspberry Surprise

**Preparation time:** 15 minutes, plus chilling

Serves 4

4 tablespoons very strong espresso coffee
2 tablespoons grappa or brandy
10 sponge fingers
125 g (4 oz, 1 cup) raspberries
175 g (6 oz) mascarpone cheese
2 eggs, separated
50 g (2 oz, ½ cup) icing sugar
25 g (1 oz) plain chocolate
mint leaves, to decorate

**1** Combine the coffee and grappa or brandy. Dip the sponge fingers into the liquid to coat them evenly, then arrange them in a small, shallow dish or a serving platter, pouring any excess liquid over them. Sprinkle the raspberries evenly over the soaked sponge fingers.

**2** In a bowl, whisk together the mascarpone, egg yolks and icing sugar until smooth and well blended.

**3** In another bowl, whisk the egg whites until stiff and glossy, then fold into the mascarpone mixture until well blended.

**4** Spoon the mixture over the sponge fingers and smooth the surface. Finely grate the chocolate straight on to the mixture. Cover and chill until set. Decorate with mint leaves.

## barbie tip
This dessert is best made the night before so that it can set completely.

# Raspberry Sorbet

**barbie tip**

For a special occasion, pour a little liqueur, such as Cointreau, cassis or framboise, over each serving.

**Preparation time:** 10 minutes, plus freezing

Serves 4–6

500 g (1 lb, 4 cups) raspberries, fresh or frozen
125 g (4 oz, ½ cup) sugar
300 ml (½ pint, 1¼ cups) water
2 egg whites

**1** Thaw the raspberries at room temperature for 3–4 hours if you are using them from the freezer. Pass the raspberries through a sieve.

**2** Put the sugar and water in a saucepan and stir over a gentle heat until the sugar has dissolved. Increase the heat and boil briskly, without stirring, for 8 minutes or until a syrup has formed. Allow to cool.

**3** Stir the syrup into the raspberry purée and pour into an ice tray or shallow rigid container. Place in the freezer for 1 hour or until just smooth. Whisk the egg whites until stiff and fold into the raspberry mixture.

**4** Thaw the sorbet in the refrigerator for 10–15 minutes before serving.

# Champagne Syllabub with Strawberries

**Preparation time:** 5–10 minutes, plus chilling

Serves 4

150 ml (¼ pint, ⅔ cup) Champagne or dry
   sparkling wine
2 tablespoons caster sugar
finely grated rind and juice of ½ lemon
300 ml (½ pint, 1¼ cups) double cream
ripe strawberries, to serve

**1** Mix the Champagne, sugar, lemon rind and
juice together in a large bowl.

**2** Add the cream and whisk the mixture until
it forms soft peaks. Spoon into glasses and
chill for 1–2 hours. Serve with ripe

### barbie tip
For a special touch, serve with
a mixture of cultivated and wild
strawberries.

strawberries.

# chapter 10
# Marinades and More

Add extra flavour to your barbecue with this
selection of marinades, sauces and salad dressings.

## Herb Marinade

This marinade is particularly good with fish such as tuna or mackerel.

**Preparation time:** 5 minutes

**Serves 4**

4 tablespoons olive oil
4 garlic cloves, crushed
125 ml (4 fl oz, ½ cup ) dry white wine
1 small onion, finely chopped
1 sprig each of rosemary, thyme and parsley

**1** Mix all the ingredients together and marinate the fish for several hours or overnight.

## Soy Sauce Marinade

This marinade works especially well with tuna, salmon and halibut steaks.

**Preparation time:** 5 minutes

**Serves 4**

2 tablespoons oil
2 tablespoons light soy sauce
1 tablespoon lemon juice
½ teaspoon ground cumin
1 teaspoon chopped chives

**1** Mix all the marinade ingredients together. Pour over the fish and leave to marinate in the mixture for at least 30 minutes, or overnight. Use the marinade to baste the fish while cooking.

## Hoisin Marinade

Use this marinade to flavour fish or chicken.

**Preparation time:** 5 minutes

**Serves 4**

125 ml (4 fl oz, ½ cup) hoisin sauce
3 tablespoons tomato purée
2 tablespoons lemon juice
2 tablespoons honey
2 tablespoons soy sauce

**1** Combine all the marinade ingredients together and pour them over the fish or chicken. Leave to marinate for at least 30 minutes.

## Teriyaki Marinade

Use this marinade for chicken, salmon and prawns.

**Preparation time:** 5 minutes

**Serves 4**

2 cm (¾ inch) piece fresh root ginger, finely grated
2 tablespoons soy sauce
1 tablespoon lemon juice
2 tablespoons dry sherry
125 ml (4 fl oz, ½ cup) fish stock

**1** In a shallow dish combine all the ingredients for the marinade. Marinate the food for at least 30 minutes, turning occasionally.

## Coconut Cream Marinade

Preparation time: 5 minutes

Serves 4

2 garlic cloves, crushed
1 cm (½ inch) piece fresh root ginger, peeled and very
   finely shredded
2 tablespoons lime juice
2 teaspoons grated lemon rind
1–2 red chillies, deseeded and finely chopped
125 ml (4 fl oz, ½ cup) coconut cream

**1** Mix together all the marinade ingredients
and place in a dish with the food. Leave to
marinate for 1–2 hours.

## Barbecue Marinade

Preparation time: 5 minutes

Serves 6

1 teaspoon mustard powder
1 teaspoon salt
½ teaspoon chilli powder
1 tablespoon firmly packed dark brown sugar
300 g (10 oz, 1¼ cups) can condensed tomato soup
2 tablespoons vinegar
2 tablespoons Worcestershire sauce
2 tablespoons soy sauce

**1** Mix all the marinade ingredients together
and pour over ribs, chops or chicken to cover.
Leave in a cool place to marinade for at least
1–2 hours.

## Sweet and Sour Marinade

Preparation time: 5 minutes

Serves 4

4 tablespoons tomato ketchup
2 tablespoons Worcestershire sauce
2 tablespoons white wine vinegar
2 tablespoons honey
2 tablespoons soft brown sugar

**1** Mix together all the ingredients. Place the
food in a shallow dish and brush with the
marinade, cover and refrigerate for 4 hours, or
preferably overnight.

## Vermouth Marinade

Preparation time: 5 minutes

Serves 6–8

50 ml (2 fl oz, ¼ cup) olive oil
50 ml (2 fl oz, ¼ cup) dry vermouth
1 tablespoon lemon juice
1 garlic clove, crushed
1 teaspoon Worcestershire sauce
few drops of angostura bitters
pepper

**1** Combine all the ingredients, with black
pepper to taste, in a bowl and beat lightly
together. Use to marinade in a cool place (not
the refrigerator) for at least 1 hour.

# Chermoula

Preparation time: 10 minutes

Serves 6

2 teaspoons cumin seeds
1 teaspoon coriander seeds
½ teaspoon crushed dried chillies
3 garlic cloves, crushed
finely grated rind and juice of 1 lime
3 tablespoons olive oil
15 g (½ oz, 1 tablespoon) mixed coriander and
    parsley, chopped
salt

**1** Lightly pound the cumin and coriander seeds using a pestle and mortar (or a small bowl and the end of a rolling pin). Mix in a bowl with the remaining ingredients and use to coat fish before barbecuing.

# Mixed Herb Butter

Preparation time: 5 minutes, plus chilling

Serves 6

75 g (3 oz, ¼ cup plus 2 tablespoons) butter
½ tablespoon chopped tarragon
½ tablespoon chopped chervil
½ tablespoon chopped dill
½ tablespoon chopped chives
½ tablespoon chopped mint
1 tablespoon lemon juice
salt and pepper

**1** Blend the butter in a blender or food processor, then add the rest of the ingredients and mix well. Alternatively, beat the butter in a bowl until creamy, then add the remaining ingredients and combine.

**2** Roll the butter in greaseproof paper to form a sausage shape, then chill until firm.

# Aromatic Oil

Preparation time: 10 minutes, plus standing

Makes 450 ml (¾ pint, 1¾ cups)

450 ml (¾ pint, 1¾ cups) olive oil
2 large rosemary sprigs
6 thyme sprigs
1 large garlic clove, halved
1 green chilli
5–6 small red chillies
6 black peppercorns
6 juniper berries

**1** Pour the oil into a clear glass bottle with a tightly fitting lid or cork. Wash the herbs thoroughly and dry with kitchen paper.

**2** Drop the herbs into the oil with the remaining ingredients and seal tightly.

**3** Allow the oil to stand for 2 weeks before using it, shaking the bottle every 2 or 3 days.

# Salmoriglio Sauce

Preparation time: 10 minutes

Serves 4

175 ml (6 fl oz, ¾ cup) extra virgin olive oil
5 tablespoons lemon juice
2 teaspoons dried oregano
2 garlic cloves, finely chopped
2 tablespoons chopped parsley

**1** Whisk all the ingredients together until thick and drizzle over barbecued fish, squid or prawns.

# Honey Sauce

**Preparation time:** 5 minutes, plus cooling
**Cooking time:** 10 minutes

**Makes 300 ml (½ pint, 1¼ cups)**

2 tablespoons oil
1 onion, finely chopped
1 garlic clove, crushed
4 tablespoons orange juice
2 tablespoons clear honey
3 tablespoons wine vinegar
1 tablespoon Worcestershire sauce
1 teaspoon horseradish sauce
1 teaspoon dry mustard
large pinch of dried rosemary
large pinch of dried thyme
salt and pepper

**1** Heat the oil in a saucepan and add the onion and garlic. Cook gently over a low heat until soft but not brown.

**2** Stir in the remaining ingredients with salt and pepper to taste and simmer for 5 minutes. Allow to cool for 4–6 hours in the refrigerator before using as a marinade or basting sauce.

# Spicy Peanut Sauce

Make this rich, spicy dressing in advance to allow the flavours to develop before using.

**Preparation time:** 10 minutes
**Cooking time:** 2 minutes

**Makes 150 ml (¼ pint, ⅔ cup)**

2 tablespoons creamed coconut
4 tablespoons milk
½ small onion, chopped
1 garlic clove, crushed
4 tablespoons smooth peanut butter
1 teaspoon soft brown sugar
2 teaspoons soy sauce
½ teaspoon ground cumin
½ teaspoon chilli powder
salt and pepper

**1** Chop the creamed coconut and place in a small pan with the milk. Heat gently for about 2 minutes, stirring constantly until the coconut melts and forms a paste with the milk.

**2** Transfer the coconut mixture to a blender or food processor and add all the remaining ingredients. Process until smooth, then transfer to a small bowl. Cover and set aside until required.

# Basic Tomato Sauce

**Preparation time:** 10 minutes
**Cooking time:** 1 hour

**Serves 4**

1 kg (2 lb) fresh ripe tomatoes, quartered, or drained
    canned whole tomatoes, roughly chopped
1 onion, finely chopped
2 garlic cloves, chopped
4 basil leaves, bruised
125 ml (4 fl oz, ½ cup) olive oil

**1** Place the tomatoes in a large saucepan with the onion and garlic. Cover the pan, bring to the boil then cook slowly for 25 minutes.

**2** Uncover the pan and simmer for another 15–30 minutes to evaporate any extra liquid, as the sauce should be quite thick.

**3** Purée the sauce in a blender or food processor, then sieve it to remove any seeds and skin. Stir in the basil and oil.

## Avocado Salsa

This tangy salsa makes a great accompaniment to warm dishes, especially as part of a buffet.

**Preparation time:** 10 minutes

**Serves 4**

1 firm, ripe avocado
2 tablespoons lime juice
1 tablespoon finely chopped coriander
2 spring onions, finely sliced
salt and pepper
diced red pepper, to garnish

**1** Cut lengthways through the centre of the avocado as far as the stone, then gently twist the two halves apart. Remove the stone, peel off the skin and cut the avocado into 1 cm (½ inch) dice.

**2** Put the avocado flesh into a bowl with the lime juice, coriander and spring onions. Season to taste with salt and pepper and toss lightly to combine without damaging the avocado. Cover and refrigerate until required. Serve garnished with diced red pepper.

## Danish Blue Dip

Serve this dip with oatcakes, breadsticks or a selection of fresh vegetables, such as carrot sticks, cauliflower and broccoli florets.

**Preparation time:** 5 minutes, plus chilling

**Serves 4**

250 g (8 oz) Danish Blue or Gorgonzola cheese, softened
350 ml (12 fl oz, 1½ cups) double cream
1 tablespoon Worcestershire sauce
salt and pepper

**1** Place the cheese and cream in a bowl. Mix together with a wooden spoon, then beat vigorously. Stir in the Worcestershire sauce and seasoning to taste. Spoon into a serving bowl and chill in the refrigerator before serving.

## Guacamole

Cover the guacamole tightly with clingfilm to prevent it discolouring in the refrigerator, and do not chill it for more than 1 hour, as any longer may cause it to lose its pretty colour.

**Preparation time:** 15 minutes, plus chilling

**Serves 6**

2 large ripe avocados
3 tablespoons lemon or lime juice
2 garlic cloves, crushed
40 g (1½ oz, 3 tablespoons) chopped spring onions
1–2 tablespoons chopped mild green chillies
2 tablespoons chopped coriander
125 g (4 oz) tomatoes, skinned, seeded and chopped
salt and pepper
tortilla chips, to serve

**1** Cut the avocados in half and remove the stones. Scoop out the flesh and sprinkle with a little of the lemon or lime juice to prevent it discolouring.

**2** Put the avocado flesh into a bowl with the remaining lemon or lime juice and mash coarsely. Add the garlic, spring onions, chillies and coriander, and season to taste with salt and pepper. Mix in the chopped tomatoes.

**3** Cover and chill in the refrigerator for 1 hour. Serve with tortilla chips.

# Mayonnaise

Preparation time: by hand 20 minutes; by blender 5 minutes

Serves 4–6

2 egg yolks (at room temperature)
1 teaspoon Dijon mustard
up to 300 ml (½ pint, 1¼ cups) virgin olive oil (at room temperature)
3 teaspoons white wine vinegar or lemon juice
1 tablespoon very hot water (optional)
salt and white pepper

**1** To make by hand, put the egg yolks into a mixing bowl and add the mustard and salt and pepper. Whisk to blend. Hold the container of oil in one hand, and leave your 'working' hand free to whisk continually.

**2** Add the oil in a very slow trickle, whisking all the time. If there is the slightest sign of the mixture curdling, stop adding the oil and whisk very hard. If that does not help, you will need to add another egg yolk.

**3** Beat this in and start adding the oil once again. The 2 egg yolks should absorb the quantity of oil specified but for many people this gives too oily a dressing, so stop when sufficient has been incorporated. Add the vinegar or lemon juice. The hot water will lighten the dressing. Use the mayonnaise at once or cover and refrigerate for 2–3 days only.

**4** To make in a blender or food processor, put the eggs into the goblet or bowl with the mustard, salt and pepper. Keep the motor running at the lowest speed possible. Gradually trickle in the oil through the feeding funnel, or space in the lid. When this has been incorporated, add the vinegar or lemon juice and hot water, if using.

# Green Mayonnaise

Preparation time: 10 minutes

Serves 6

3 egg yolks
1 tablespoon finely chopped chives
1 tablespoon finely chopped parsley
1 tablespoon lemon juice
300 ml (½ pint, 1¼ cups) olive oil
salt and pepper

**1** Place the egg yolks, herbs and lemon juice in a blender or food processor and blend for 1–2 minutes. Keeping the motor running, pour in the oil in a very thin stream until it is all incorporated. Add salt and pepper to taste.

# Pistou

This robust basil sauce can be spooned on to plain grilled fish steaks, courgettes or chicken.

Preparation time: 10 minutes

Makes 300 ml (½ pint)

3 garlic cloves, crushed
15 g (½ oz, ½ cup) basil leaves
150 ml (¼ pint, ⅔ cup) virgin olive oil
50 g (2 oz, ½ cup) walnuts or pine nuts
1 teaspoon lemon juice
50 g (2 oz) Parmesan, freshly grated
salt and pepper

**1** Put the garlic in a blender, food processor or a large pestle and mortar. Add the basil leaves and blend together roughly.

**2** Add the olive oil gradually, to make a fresh green purée. Add the walnuts or pine nuts, salt if necessary, black pepper and lemon juice. Blend together briefly. Stir in the Parmesan.

## Blue Cheese Dressing

Preparation time: 5 minutes

Makes 300 ml (½ pint, 1¼ cups)

125 g (4 oz) blue cheese, such as Danish Blue or
    Cashel Blue, crumbled
125 ml (4 fl oz, ½ cup) Mayonnaise (see page 187)
125 ml (4 fl oz, ½ cup) double cream
large pinch of salt
½ teaspoon pepper

**1** Combine all the ingredients in a mixing
bowl, beating until thoroughly combined.
Store the dressing in the refrigerator until
ready to use.

## Classic Vinaigrette

Preparation time: 5 minutes

Makes 250 ml (8 fl oz, 1 cup)

175 ml (6 fl oz, ¾ cup) olive oil
4 tablespoons white wine vinegar, cider vinegar or
    tarragon vinegar
1 teaspoon clear honey
2 tablespoons chopped mixed herbs (such as mint,
    parsley, chives, thyme)
1 garlic clove, crushed
salt and pepper

**1** Beat the oil with the vinegar, honey, herbs,
garlic, and salt and pepper to taste until well
blended. Alternatively, place all the ingredients
in a screw-top jar and shake vigorously to
combine will before using.

## Honey Dressing

Preparation time: 5 minutes

Makes 125 ml (4 fl oz, ½ cup)

4 tablespoons lemon juice
2 tablespoons clear honey
3 tablespoons olive oil
salt and pepper

**1** Beat together the lemon juice, honey, olive
oil, and salt and pepper to taste until well
blended. Alternatively, place all the ingredients
in a screw-top jar and shake vigorously to
combine well before use.

## Mint Dressing

This light and refreshing dressing would taste
delicious with a cold potato salad or tossed
lightly over a salad of green leaves.

Preparation time: 5 minutes, plus standing

Makes 125 ml (4 fl oz, ½ cup)

6 tablespoons olive oil
2 tablespoons lemon juice
2–3 tablespoons chopped mint
pinch of sugar
salt and pepper

**1** Beat the oil with the lemon juice, mint,
sugar, and salt and pepper to taste until well
blended. Alternatively, place all the ingredients
in a screw-top jar and shake vigorously to
combine well before serving.

**2** Set aside for at least 15 minutes to allow
the flavours to develop, then beat or shake
again before testing.

## Soy Sauce Dressing

Preparation time: 5 minutes

Makes 300 ml (½ pint, 1¼ cups)

250 ml (8 fl oz, 1 cup) corn oil
4 tablespoons soy sauce
2 tablespoons lemon juice
1 garlic clove, crushed
salt and pepper

**1** Beat together the corn oil, soy sauce, lemon juice, garlic, and salt and pepper to taste. Alternatively, place all the ingredients in a screw-top jar and shake vigorously to combine well before using.

## Pesto Dressing

Preparation time: 5 minutes

Makes 250 ml (8 fl oz, 1 cup)

25 g (1 oz, 1 cup) basil leaves
3 tablespoons grated Parmesan cheese
1 tablespoon pine nuts
4 tablespoons white wine vinegar
1 garlic clove, crushed
125 ml (4 fl oz, ½ cup) extra virgin olive oil
pepper

**1** Combine the basil leaves, Parmesan, pine nuts, vinegar and garlic in a blender or food processor. Season with black pepper to taste. Process for a few seconds.

**2** With the blender or food processor running, add the olive oil through the feeder tube in a thin, steady stream, until the mixture becomes thick and smooth. Pour into a bowl or jug and use as required.

## Caesar Dressing

Preparation time: 5 minutes

Serves 4–6

5 tablespoons Mayonnaise (see page 187)
4–5 tablespoons water
1–2 garlic cloves
3 tablespoons finely grated Parmesan cheese
coarse sea salt and pepper

**1** Put the mayonnaise in a small bowl and stir in enough of the water to make a thin, pourable sauce. Pound the garlic to a paste with a little coarse sea salt. Add to the mayonnaise along with the Parmesan and stir well. Thin it with a little more water, if necessary, so that the sauce remains pourable. Add pepper to taste and set aside.

## Thousand Island Dressing

Preparation time: 10 minutes, plus standing

Makes 350 ml (12 fl oz, 1½ cups)

½ quantity Mayonnaise (see page 187)
½ teaspoon paprika
1 teaspoon grated onion
pinch of garlic salt
½ teaspoon tomato purée
2 teaspoons chopped parsley
3 tablespoons finely chopped red pepper
3 tablespoons finely chopped green pepper
2 tablespoons finely chopped celery
2 green olives or 1 small gherkin, finely chopped

**1** Mix the mayonnaise with the paprika, onion, garlic salt and tomato purée in a bowl. Add the parsley, peppers, celery and olives or gherkin, and mix well to blend. Set aside for at least 15 minutes to allow the flavours to develop before using.

# Index

# Acknowledgements

**Executive Editor:** Nicola Hill
**Editor:** Abi Rowsell
**Executive Art Editor:** Leigh Jones
**Designer:** Jo Tapper
**Senior Production Controller:** Louise Hall
**Picture Researcher:** Jennifer Veall
**Special Photography:** Dave Jordan/Jeremy Hopley
**Stylists:** Judy Williams/Clare Hunt

## Photographic Acknowledgements

Leigh Jones 4 bottom right, 4 bottom centre left, 4 bottom centre right, 5 bottom right, 22, 28, 64, 82, 139, 154, 165, 166, 176, 180, 181
Octopus Publishing Group Limited/Octopus Publishing Group Limited/Bryce Attwell 15, 18/Jean Cazals 29, 37, 58/Stephen Conroy 31/Gus Filgate 146/Jeremy Hopley 2, 3, 5 Top, 8, 9, 27, 47, 49, 52, 53, 65, 71, 79, 83, 85, 91, 92, 106, 107, 115, 116, 123, 127, 131, 135, 143, 145, 149, 158, 168/Dave Jordan 1, 4 bottom centre, 5 bottom centre left, 39, 41, 46, 122, 124, 132/Sandra Lane 32/William Lingwood 157, 178/David Loftus 73, 151, 155/James Merrell 5 bottom centre, 5 bottom centre right, 23, 24, 26, 33, 35, 40, 50, 51, 55, 59, 60, 61, 66, 69, 75, 86, 87, 88, 89, 94, 97, 99, 110, 118, 133, 136, 137, 138, 142, 152, 153, 160, 162, 163, 164, 167, 169, 170, 174, 179/Neil Mersh 4 bottom left, 14, 21, 72, 76, 103, 113/Hilary Moore 11, 17, 42, 54, 95, 98, 111, 129/Alan Newnham 20, 108/William Reavell 5 bottom left, 102, 117, 120, 161/Ian Wallace 57, 77, 105, 119, 172, 177/Philip Webb 36